997
7.21

Walking with God

A made easy handbook

on Spiritual Disciplines

Mark Water

HENDRICKSON
PUBLISHERS

Walking with God
Hendrickson Publishers, Inc.
P.O. Box 3473
Peabody, Massachusetts 01961-3473

ISBN 1-56563-982-0

A compilation of five titles in
the Made Easy range:
Prayer made easy
 – first printing 1999
Daily Devotions made easy
 – first printing 1999
Scripture Memory made easy
 – first printing 1999
Sharing Your Faith made easy
 – first printing 1999
Knowing God's Will made easier
 – first printing 1998

Designed and produced
by Tony Cantale Graphics

First printing — September 2003

Manufactured in China

Photography supplied by Foxx
Photos, Goodshoot, Digital Vision,
Photo Alto and Tony Cantale

Illustrations by
Tony Cantale Graphics

Prayer
made easy

Ruth Graham has been frank enough to admit that, "God has not always answered my prayers. If He had, I would have married the wrong man – several times!"

There is much to learn about the dynamics and philosophy of prayer.

But *Prayer made easy* concentrates on more down to earth topics. It answers questions like, "How can I start a life of prayer?," "How can I improve my flagging prayer life?"

Martin Luther is often quoted as having said, "I am going to be so busy today that I must spend three hours in prayer," but most of us are struggling to spend 5 or 10 minutes a day in prayer. *Prayer made easy* explains how we can pray more frequently and more effectively.

Introduction

The Made Easy series titles have sold around two million copies since they were first launched in 1998. Many have found them an aid in their daily walk with God, getting straight to the heart of the issues that concern us all and providing practical help in an easy-to-read format.

This is the first in a new series of Made Easy handbooks that bind together a number of related Made Easy titles providing an easy-to-use handbook on spiritual growth. It's the hope and prayer of the authors and publishers that these collections will help you, your family, and friends come closer to God and enjoy His presence.

Contents

By way of introduction

Prayer is no optional extra

The Lord Jesus Christ taught that prayer is not something to do when we feel like it. Rather, it is a God-given responsibility.

Why pray?

Here are some good reasons

1. Jesus told his disciples to	"Then Jesus told his disciples a parable to show them that they should always pray and not give up."	*Luke 18:1*
2. Paul said Christians should	"Devote yourselves to prayer."	*Colossians 4:2*
3. God uses prayer to bless us	"Ask and it will be given to you."	*Matthew 7:7*
4. Jesus prayed	"He [Jesus] went into the hills to pray."	*Mark 6:46*

5

A key verse to help you in your praying

See how many ways this one verse teaches us about praying.

Ephesians 6:18	**A one verse guide to prayer**
"And pray in the Spirit ...	How to pray
... on all occasions ...	When to pray
... with all kinds of prayers ...	Using a variety of prayers
... and requests. ...	Asking is part of praying
... With this in mind, be alert ...	Praying is one way to be spiritually awake
... and always keep on praying ...	Persevere in prayer
... for all the saints.	Pray for fellow Christians.

How do I get started?

The secret of praying

The secret of praying is praying. There is no hidden technique called *How to pray*. The secret is just to pray. The disciples did not ask Jesus, "Teach us *how* to pray?" They asked, "Teach us to pray."

> "One day Jesus was praying in a certain place. When he finished, one of his disciples said to him, 'Lord, teach us to pray, just as John taught his disciples.'" *Luke 11:1*

Have you ever seen a prayer rock?

It is a small rock, wrapped in attractive fabric and tied with a ribbon. On the ribbon a card is attached, and on the card are the words: "My Prayer Rock," followed by this poem.

The prayer rock poem

I'm your little prayer rock and this is what I'd do.
Just put me on your pillow until the day is through.
Then turn back the covers and climb into your bed, and
"WHACK..." your little prayer rock will hit you
    on the head.
Then you will remember as the day is through,
to kneel and say your prayers as you wanted to.
Then when you are finished just dump me on the floor.
I'll stay there through the night to give you help once more.
When you get up in the morning "CLUNK,"
    I'll stub your toe,
So you will remember your morning prayers before you go.
Put me back upon your pillow when your bed is made.
Your clever little prayer rock will continue in your aid.
Because your heavenly Father cares and loves you so,
He wants you to remember to talk to him, you know!
Author unknown

Use an alarm clock

Many Christians find that the morning is the best time to pray. For some people the most important thing in their prayer life is an alarm clock.

If you don't get up in time to have an unhurried period of prayer, don't be surprised that you skip prayer throughout the day. Hence the need for an alarm clock.

> "Very early in the morning, while it was still dark, Jesus got up, left the house and went off to a solitary place, where he prayed."
> *Mark 1:35*

A. C. T. S.

So, you've made it!

You've actually got up in time
to pray. Well done! That's more
than some Christians ever manage to do!

What do you do now? These next ten pages give a simple
outline you may wish to follow. If you do, you will cover some
of the most important areas of prayer.

A. C. T. S.

A. C. T. S. stands for the Acts of the Apostles, with each letter
representing a different aspect of prayer.
A = Adoration (or worshiping God)
C = Confession of sins to God
T = Thanksgiving
S = Supplication, asking for things in prayer

Think about whom you are praying to

Try and lose yourself in prayer, as you focus on God.
This is how the writer to the Hebrews advises us to approach
God.

"Therefore, since we have a great
high priest who has gone through
the heavens, Jesus the Son of
God, let us hold firmly to the faith
we profess. For we do not have a
high priest who is unable to
sympathize with our weaknesses,
but we have one who has been
tempted in every way, just as we
are – yet was without sin. Let us
then approach the throne of grace
with confidence, so that we may
receive mercy and find grace to
help us in our time of need."
Hebrews 4:14-16

8

A PRAYER TO
PRAY

GOD BE IN MY HEAD,
AND IN MY
UNDERSTANDING;
GOD BE IN MY EYES,
AND IN MY LOOKING;
GOD BE IN MY MOUTH,
AND IN MY SPEAKING;
GOD BE IN MY HEART,
AND IN MY THINKING;
GOD BE AT MY END,
AND AT MY DEPARTING.
Sixteenth-century Sarum Primer

9

A is for adoration

Adoration
This is a time to remember who God is.
Praise him:
> for his love,
> his power,
> his majesty,
>> and for his wonderful gift of Jesus.

Hum a hymn
You may like to sing a chorus like *Majesty* or a traditional hymn like *How Great Thou Art* or *A Mighty Fortress is Our God*.

This will help you to worship God as you start your time of prayer. It helps you to remember God's greatness and your own dependence on him.

Music
You may try playing a track of Christian music from a CD or cassette.

Using a hymn book
At the beginning of your time of prayer, try praying one hymn a day from the Praise or Worship section of a hymn book.

Some psalms of worship
Turn to a psalm to help your spirit as a means to start praising God. Try one of these each day, for a month.

Psalm number
19; 29; 33; 34; 35; 47; 50; 76; 87; 91; 93;
95; 96; 99; 100; 104; 107; 111; 113; 114; 115; 117;
121; 134; 139; 145; 146; 147; 148; 150.

Psalm 117
"Praise the Lord, all you nations;
> extol him, all you peoples.
For great is his love towards us,
> and the faithfulness of the Lord endures for ever.
Praise the Lord."
Psalm 117:1-2

An acrostic on P-R-A-Y-E-R

Prayer is made up of:

PETITION:	"He [Daniel] still prays three times a day."	*Daniel 6:13*
REVERENCE:	"Worship God acceptably with reverence and awe."	*Hebrews 12:28*
ADORATION:	"My lips will glorify you."	*Psalm 63:3*
YEARNING:	"Blessed are those who hunger and thirst after righteousness."	*Matthew 5:6*
EXPECTATION:	"Elijah ... prayed earnestly that it might not rain."	*James 5:17*
REQUESTS:	"Present your requests to God."	*Philippians 4:6*

C is for confessing sin

Confessing sin to God

It's not as if you are telling God anything he does not already know when you admit to him your sins. But it does show that you are sorry for them and that you really do want his forgiveness and are determined (with his help) not to keep on repeating the same old sins, day after day.

This time of owning up to your sin is a time to be honest and humble.

God never stops loving you, no matter how sinful you have been. Be reassured about this. Read Luke 15:11-32 and focus on the love of the father in this story of the prodigal son.

Remember: God loves you like that.

A SAYING ABOUT PRAYER

"MORE THINGS ARE WROUGHT BY PRAYER THAN THIS WORLD DREAMS OF."
Lord Alfred Tennyson

Peter's advice, quoting Psalm 34

"For the eyes of the Lord are on the righteous
   and his ears are attentive to their prayer,
but the face of the Lord is against those who do evil."
1 Peter 3:12

There is only one way to be righteous in God's sight, and that is to confess our sin to him and to accept as a gift the righteousness of Jesus.

God's assures us that he will forgive us

"If we claim to be without sin, we deceive ourselves and the truth is not in us. If we confess our sins, he [God] is faithful and just and will forgive us our sins and purify us from all unrighteousness."
1 John 1:9

Confess your sin before you pray for others

The order in which you pray is not important. We move constantly between adoration, confession, thanksgiving and supplication. But if we want God to hear and answer our prayers we need to confess and let go of our own sin.

A wonderful promise

Buried deep in the Old Testament is this wonderful promise that if we confess our sin to God he will listen to and answer our prayers.

"If my people, who are called by
my name,
will humble themselves
and pray
and seek my face
and *turn from their wicked ways*,
then I will hear them from
heaven and will forgive their
sin and will heal their land."

2 Chronicles 7:14

A PRAYER TO
PRAY

THE JESUS PRAYER
LORD JESUS CHRIST, SON OF GOD,
HAVE MERCY ON ME, A SINNER.
*For many centuries Eastern Orthodox
Christians have used this prayer as a basis
for their praying and daily living.*

T is for thanksgiving

Thanksgiving

Before you start thinking about what you are going to pray for, spend some moments in giving thanks to God.

"Give thanks in all circumstances."
1 Thessalonians 5:18

"Give thanks to the Lord ... remember the wonders he has done." *Psalm 104:1,5*

Thank God for his forgiveness

Praise the Lord, O my soul,
  and forget not all his benefits –
who forgives all your sins
  and heals all your diseases, ...
For as high as the heavens are above the earth,
  so great is his love for those who fear him;
as far as the east is from the west,
  so far has he removed our transgressions from us.
Psalm 103:2-3, 11-12

14

Why and when we are to give thanks to God

1. As we approach him.	"Let us come before him with thanksgiving."	*Psalm 95:2*
2. For the gift of Jesus.	"Thanks be to God for his indescribable gift!"	*2 Corinthians 9:15*
3. Because God is good.	"Give thanks to the Lord, for he is good."	*Psalm 136:1*
4. For deliverance from sin's grip.	"I see ... the law of sin at work within my members. What a wretched man I am! Who will rescue me from this body of death? Thanks be to God – through Jesus Christ our Lord!	*Romans 7:23-25*
5. All of God's good gifts.	"For everything God created is good, and nothing is to be rejected if it is received with thanksgiving, because it is consecrated by the word of God and prayer."	*1 Timothy 4:4-5*
6. The defeat of death and sin.	"But thanks be to God! He gives us the victory through our Lord Jesus Christ."	*1 Corinthians 15:57*
7. Give thanks continually.	"Through Jesus, therefore, let us continually offer to God a sacrifice of praise."	*Hebrews 13:15*

Only one in ten bothered to say "thank you"

Jesus healed ten lepers, see Luke 17:11-19, but only one went back to Jesus to thank him.

> "One of them, when he saw he was healed, came back, praising God in a loud voice. He threw himself at Jesus' feet and thanked him – and he was a Samaritan."
> *Luke 17:16*

S is for supplication

Supplication

This is the time to make specific requests in prayer, both for others and for yourself.

Four prayer topics from the Bible	
1. The sick	*James 5:14-16*
2. Rulers	*1 Timothy 2:1-3*
3. More Christian workers	"Jesus went through all the towns and villages, teaching in their synagogues, preaching the good news of the kingdom and healing every disease and sickness. When he saw the crowds, he had compassion on them, because they were harassed and helpless, like sheep without a shepherd. Then he said to his disciples, 'The harvest is plentiful but the workers are few. Ask the Lord of the harvest, therefore, to send out workers into his harvest field.'" *Matthew 9:35-38*
4. Yourself	*1 Chronicles 4:10; Psalm 106:4-5*

David Brainerd

The Life and Dairy of David Brainerd, published after his death by his friend Jonathan Edwards, has probably influenced more revivals than any other book. His life was one of burning prayer for the American Indians. Brainerd was converted at the age of twenty-one and immediately became a pioneer missionary. He spent six years of astonishing, agonizing prayer until, in 1744, when he was twenty-seven, a remarkable revival swept over his work.

Brainerd's Journal

The following extract from Brainerd's journal was written in 1742, when he had been a Christian for three years and was twenty-four years old.

"I set apart this day for secret fasting and prayer, to entreat God to direct and bless me with regard to the great work I have in view, of preaching the gospel. Just last night the Lord visited me marvelously in prayer: I think my soul never was in such an agony before. I felt no restraint; for the treasures of divine grace were opened before me.

I wrestled for absent friends, for the ingathering of souls, and for the children of God in many distant places. I was in such agony, from sun half an hour high, till near dark, that I was all over wet with sweat. Oh, my dear Jesus did sweat blood for poor souls! I longed for more compassion towards them."

Pray through your day

Go through your day in prayer asking for God's special help over the worrisome things or anything that you are dreading.

A SAYING ABOUT
PRAYER
TALKING TO PEOPLE ABOUT GOD IS A GREAT PRIVILEGE, BUT TALKING TO GOD FOR PEOPLE IS GREATER STILL.

Does God always answer our requests?

God always gives an answer – but sometimes it may be "no," or "wait," or "I have a better way." This is what Paul found out. *See 2 Corinthians 12:9-10*

Where and to whom should I pray?

Who am I praying to?

Many people think of God as:

- a distant tyrant
- a sort of slot-machine
- an impersonal force

When we pray we are talking to a good and loving Father – the sort of Father all our fathers ought to copy.

Loving Father

1. A loving Father	"Which of you fathers, if your son asks for a fish, will give him a snake instead? Or if he asks for an egg, will give him a scorpion?"	*Luke 11:11*
	"If you, then, though you are evil, know how to give good gifts to your children, how much more will your Father in heaven give good gifts to those who ask him!"	*Matthew 7:11*
2. Your Father	"To all who received him ... he gave the right to become children of God."	*John 1:12*

Where to pray

1. In private	"But when your pray, go into your room, close the door and pray to your Father, who is unseen."	*Matthew 6:6*
2. In public	"So they took away the stone. [Just before the raising of Lazarus.] Jesus looked up and said, 'Father, I thank you that you have heard me. I knew that your always hear me, but I said this for the benefit of the people standing here, that they may believe that you send me."	*John 11:42*
3. Anywhere	"Pray continually."	*1 Thessalonians 5:17*

Wherever you are

1. As you wake	Let your waking thoughts turn to thank God for his goodness and for a new day. "When I awake I am still with you."	*Psalm 139:18*
2. As you wash and dress	As you wash let the running water be a symbol of God's cleansing and his refreshment of your soul. As you dress say over in your mind or aloud a phrase from a Bible verse you know. Or, think about one of Jesus' kind actions recorded in the Gospels.	
3. In the middle of the day	Snatch a moment to be quiet in your mind. Recall a promise of Jesus, like, "I am with you always."	*Matthew 28:20*
4. As you go to sleep	Make a promise to God as you lay on your pillow to rest. "I will lie down and sleep in peace, for you alone, O Lord, make me dwell in safety."	*Psalm 4:8*
5. If you are wakeful	Try repeating over and over again a Bible verse or part of a verse, about God's comfort. "The Lord is my shepherd, I shall not be in want."	*Psalm 23:1*

When and how and what should I pray?

Set times for prayer

There's no one rule about this. Many Christians like to pray first thing in the morning and last thing at night.

In addition, some people try to follow the practice of short periods of prayer at 6 AM, 9 AM, 12 noon, 3 PM, 6 PM, 9 PM, and 12 midnight.

"Seven times a day I praise you." *Psalm 119:164*

Should I kneel when I pray?

You can kneel, sit, stand, or raise your hands. It really doesn't matter. Prayer is meant to be a time when we express our dependence on God. Many Christians find that kneeling helps them to do this.

How did people pray in the Bible?

1. They often knelt	"Come let us bow down in worship, let us kneel before the Lord our Maker."	*Psalm 95:6*
	"Every knee will bow before me; every tongue will confess to God."	*Romans 14:11*
	"... and there on the beach we knelt to pray."	*Acts 21:5*
2. They lifted up their hands	"Lift up your hands in the sanctuary and praise the Lord."	*Psalm 134:2*
	"I will praise you as long as I live, and in your name I will lift up my hands."	*Psalm 63:4*
	"I urge, then, first of all, that requests, prayers, intercession and thanksgiving be made for everyone ... I want men everywhere to lift up holy hands in prayer."	*1 Timothy 2:1,8*

What should I pray for?

If you want to pray for the same kinds of things that the early Christians prayed for, go through a New Testament letter and see what the writer prayed for and what he asked prayer for.

10 Prayer topics in the Acts of the Apostles

Topic	Reference in Acts
1. Prayer for unity	1:14
2. Prayer to know God's will	1:24
3. Prayer in church services	3:1
4. Prayer linked to preaching	6:4
5. Prayer for new Christians	8:15
6. Prayer for persecuted Christians	12:5
7. Prayer for missionaries	13:2-4
8. Prayer when in severe trouble	16:25
9. Prayer for Christian leaders	21:5
10. Prayer for healing	28:8

Praying on your own

Praying in the Spirit

All true prayer is praying in the Spirit.

For you either pray just using your own efforts or else you pray in the Spirit, with the help of the Holy Spirit.

> "But you, dear friends, build yourselves up in your most holy faith and pray in the Holy Spirit." *Jude 20*

> "And pray in the Spirit ..." *Ephesians 6:18*

A book of prayers

Try praying one prayer a day from a book of traditional or contemporary prayers.

Coping with distractions

For some people, like mothers with toddlers, there is hardly five minutes of calm and quiet in the day or even through the night!

Don't worry if you're unable to have a long time of quiet for prayer. You can still pray short prayers (sometimes called *sentence prayers*) to God through your day. Remember: Jesus understands. He grew up in a large family. He had at least four younger half-brothers and at least two younger half-sisters.

> "Isn't this the carpenter? Isn't this Mary's son and the brother of James, Joseph, Judas and Simon? Aren't his sisters here with us?" *Mark 6:3*

But even without the demands of a family, some people find that their thoughts begin to wander as soon as they start to pray. If you find that you start to think about things you had forgotten, keep a pencil and paper at hand to write these things down. Then you can forget them until you have finished praying.

Are my prayers being heard?

Most Christians have wondered about this. We have Jesus's promises to rest on – nothing more and nothing less.

> "Until now you have not asked for anything in my name. Ask and you will receive, and your joy will be complete."
> *John 16:24*

Spiritual warfare

Remember: prayer is a great spiritual battle. The last thing in the world Satan wants you to be able to do is to have a time when you pray to God.

Jesus is interested in you and your needs

Think positively. The Lord Jesus Christ is your Savior and Friend. So you have the unique privilege of speaking directly with your heavenly Father through him.

Paul says to pray like this:

> "Do not be anxious about anything, but in everything, by prayer and petition, with thanksgiving, present your requests to God."
> *Philippians 4:6*

A PRAYER TO **PRAY**

O LORD, YOU KNOW HOW BUSY I MUST BE THIS DAY. IF I FORGET YOU, DO NOT FORGET ME.
*General Lord Astley (1579-1652)
before the battle of Edgehill*

Praying in a small group

The Acts 2:42 model

The first Christians did not just pray as isolated individuals – they encouraged each other as they prayed together.

Acts 2:42	Lessons to learn
"They devoted themselves ...	They took their spiritual life very seriously
... to the apostles' teaching ...	They wanted to build up their faith with teaching.
... and to the fellowship ...	They kept in close contact with fellow Christians.
... to the breaking of the bread ...	They remembered Jesus' death and resurrection
... and to prayer."	Prayer was essential to them.

Prayer partners

Some churches and college fellowships encourage people to pray with one or two other Christians. In two's they are called prayer partners; in three's they are called prayer triplets, etc.

Seek out a small prayer group or a be a third of a prayer triplet!

A word of warning

It's easy to operate independently and free of restraints in small groups where no one can read your mind or see your heart.

To talk spiritually is one thing – to be spiritual is something altogether different. You need to be just as spiritually alert in a small group as in a large congregation. Jesus warned against such hypocrisy:

> "These people honor me with their lips but their hearts are far from me." *Matthew 15:8*

The way to stop yourself from being careless about prayer, either on your own or with other people, is to ask God to keep you humble.

> "This is the one I esteem:
> he who is humble and contrite in spirit,
> and trembles at my word."
> *Isaiah 66:2*

The Bible and prayer

Praying and reading the Bible should always be linked. You should pray before, during and after you read the Bible. You should expect God to speak to you as you read, and then pray about what he has said.

Our experience at these times should be like that of the two disciples who walked to Emmaus with the risen Lord Jesus.

> "Were not our hearts burning within us while he talked with us on the road and opened the Scriptures to us?" *Luke 24:32*

For how long should I pray?

There is no set time length to aim at

It's best to start small. Try setting aside five minutes a day. It's better to manage a short time of prayer than to be continually failing to pray for a longer period.

After a while you will doubtless find that you *want* to pray for longer than five minutes a day.

All night?

> "One of those days Jesus went out to a mountainside to pray, and spent the night praying to God." *Luke 6:12*

This was unusual. It was also for a specific reason.

> "When morning came, he called his disciples to him and chose twelve of them." *Luke 6:13*

Persistence in prayer

On many occasions Jesus taught that his followers should persist in prayer.

> "Ask and it will be given to you; seek and you will find; knock and the door will be opened to you. For everyone who asks receives; he who seeks finds; and to him who knocks, the door will be opened." *Matthew 7:7-8*

A SAYING ABOUT PRAYER

"AND WHEN YOU PRAY, DO NOT KEEP ON BABBLING LIKE THE PAGANS, FOR THEY THINK THEY WILL BE HEARD FOR THEIR MANY WORDS." *Matthew 6:7*

He waited for twenty years

There was one man in the Old Testament who had to wait twenty years for his prayer to be answered.

> "This is the account of Abraham's son Isaac. Abraham became the father of Isaac, and Isaac was forty years old when he married Rebekah daughter of Bethuel the Aramean from Paddan Aram and sister of Laban the Aramean. Isaac prayed to the Lord on behalf of his wife, because she was barren. The Lord answered his prayer, and his wife Rebekah became pregnant. ... Isaac was sixty years old when Rebekah gave birth." *Genesis 25:19-21, 26*

Points to note

1. Isaac was forty when he was married.
2. Rebekah was barren.
3. Isaac was sixty when Rebekah became pregnant.

A PRAYER TO
PRAY

O MOST MERCIFUL REDEEMER,
FRIEND AND BROTHER,
MAY WE KNOW YOU MORE CLEARLY,
LOVE YOU MORE DEARLY,
AND FOLLOW YOU MORE NEARLY,
DAY BY DAY.
Richard of Chichester

The Jesus prayer

The disciple's prayer

The Lord's prayer has been given many names: *The Lord's Prayer; The Jesus Prayer; The Our Father; Pater Noster* (the first two words in Latin, translating "Our Father"); *The Christian's Model Prayer*. It has also been called *The Disciple's Prayer*.

When we pray the Lord's Prayer, we come:

1. As God's children	*Our Father*
2. As worshipers	*Hallowed be your name*
3. As subject	*Your kingdom come*
4. As servants	*Your will be done*
5. As recipients	*Give us this day our daily bread*
6. As sinners	*Forgive us our sins*
7. As tempted ones	*Lead us not into temptation*
8. As victorious people	*But deliver us from the evil one*

Try praying through the Lord's Prayer, slowly, taking up to a minute per petition, remembering all the different "people" you are.

I cannot say

I cannot say "our" if I live only for myself.

I cannot say "Father" if I do not endeavor each day to act like his child.

I cannot say "in heaven" if I am laying up no treasure there.

I cannot say "hallowed be your name" if I am not striving for holiness.

I cannot say "your kingdom come" if I am not doing all in my power to hasten that wonderful event.

I cannot say "your will be done" if I am disobedient to his word.

I cannot say "on earth as it is in heaven" if I'll not serve him here and now.

I cannot say "give us today our daily bread" if I am dishonest or seeking things by subterfuge.

I cannot say "forgive us our debts" if I harbor a grudge against anyone.

I cannot say "lead us not into temptation" if I deliberately place myself in its path.

I cannot say "deliver us from evil" if I do not put on the whole armor of God.

I cannot say "yours is the kingdom" if I do not give the King the loyalty due him from a faithful subject.

I cannot attribute to him "the power" if I fear what men may do.

I cannot ascribe to him "the glory" if I'm seeking honor only for myself.

And I cannot say "for ever" if the horizon of my life is bounded completely by time.

Author unknown

Our Father in heaven

A heavenly Father

God the Father is our heavenly Father and he cares for us.

> "Therefore I tell you, do not worry about your life, what you will eat or drink; or about your body, what you will wear. Is not life more important than food, and the body more important than clothes?

> "Look at the birds of the air; they do not sow or reap or store away in barns, and yet your heavenly Father feeds them. Are you not much more valuable than they?

> "Who of you by worrying can add a single hour to his life?"
> *Matthew 6:25-28*

A SAYING ABOUT PRAYER

"IN PRAYER IT IS BETTER TO HAVE A HEART WITHOUT WORDS THAN WORDS WITHOUT A HEART."
John Bunyan

Father

The Greek word Jesus uses for "Father" in the Lord's Prayer is *pater*.

When Jesus prayed to his Father in the Garden of Gethsemane he used another word for Father, as well as *pater*. It was the Aramaic word *Abba*. So he prayed, *"Abba, pater."*

> "'*Abba*, Father,' he said, 'everything is possible for you.'"
> *Mark 14:36*

Abba

When we are born again we are adopted into God's family and God became our spiritual Father. As the apostle Paul put it, "Because you are sons, God sent the Spirit of his Son into our hearts, the Spirit who calls out 'Abba, Father'."
Galatians 4:6

As Jesus prayed, *"Abba, pater,"* so we are to pray, *"Abba, pater."*

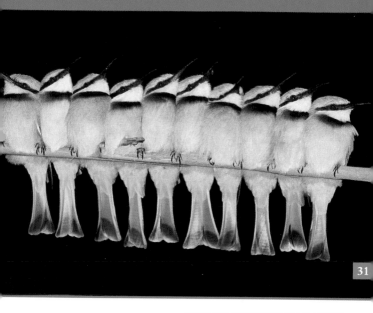

Our Father in heaven

It is not possible to translate the word *Abba* into English. Many of the Bible translations keep the word *Abba* and don't attempt any translation. At the time of Jesus it was the word a toddler called his father. Today Arab children called their father *jaba*. *Abba* is the Eastern word for Daddy.

Jesus was now telling his disciples that when they start praying they come to the God of heaven, who is so close to them that they have the privilege of praying "*our* Father in heaven."

Look at the birds of the air

Said the Robin to the Sparrow:
    "I should really like to know,
Why these anxious human beings
    Rush around and worry so?"

Said the Sparrow to the Robin:
    "Friend, I think it must be,
That they have no heavenly Father
    Such as cares for you and me!"

Hallowed be your name

Praying in the name of Jesus

Prayer must be in the name of Jesus Christ.

> "I will do whatever you ask in my name." *John 14:13*

In biblical times someone's name indicated their nature, who they were. So when we pray "in Jesus' name" we are identifying ourselves with him, having accepted his salvation.

What's in a name?

The Lord is so great that the Bible uses many different names for God to help us appreciate different aspects of his amazing nature. People have found it helpful to meditate on God's nature as revealed in adjectives associated with his name in Hebrew.

The name of the Lord

> "The name of the Lord is a strong tower, the righteous run to it and are safe."

Names linked to God

Hebrew name	English name	Bible verses to look up
1. *Shalom*	Peace, rest, contentment	*Isaiah 53:5; Hebrews 4:9-10; John 14:27; Philippians 4:7; Colossians 1:19-20* "He called it The Lord is Peace." *Judges 6:24*
2. *Zidkenu*	Righteousness, perfection	*Jeremiah 23:6; 2 Corinthians 5:21; 1 Corinthians 1:30* "For in the gospel a righteousness from God is revealed." *Romans 1:17*
3. *M'kaddesh*	Sanctifies, purifies	*Isaiah 6; 1 Corinthians 6:9-11; Romans 8:29* "May God himself ... sanctify you through and through." *1 Thessalonians 5:23*
4. *Rophe*	Heals	*Exodus 15:26.* "By his wounds you have been healed." *1 Peter 2:24*
5. *Yira*	Who sees, provides	*Psalm 34:15,18* "So Abraham called that place The Lord Will Provide." *Genesis 22:14*
6. *Nissi*	Banner, security, captain	*1 Corinthians 15:56-57* "Moses built an altar and called it The Lord is my Banner." *Exodus 17:15*
7. *Rohi*	Shepherd, companion, friend	*Proverbs 18:24; 1 Peter 2:25* "The Lord is my shepherd." *Psalm 23:1*

Hallowed

As you praise your Father God for who he is you begin to worship him, to adore God, to hallow his name.

> "Ascribe to the Lord the glory due unto His name ... Worship the Lord in the splendor of his holiness." *1 Chronicles 16:29*

Two kinds of praise and adoration

As you pray praise God for who he is and for what he has done.

> "Enter his gates with thanksgiving and his courts with praise; give thanks to him and praise his name." *Psalm 100:4*

Your kingdom come

Two thoughts about God's kingdom

God's "kingdom" means God's rule.

1. It is within Christians.	"The kingdom of God is within you."	*Luke 17:21*
2. It has priority over everything else.	"But first seek his kingdom and his righteousness, and all these things will be given to you as well.	*Matthew 6:33*

A SAYING ABOUT
PRAYER

"THY WILL BE DONE,
BY ME NOW!"
C.S. Lewis

Praying for God's kingdom to come

1. For God's worldwide church

"Your kingdom come" has been called the greatest missionary prayer ever prayed. It includes the whole world as we ask that God's rule should be extended to every part of the globe.

2. For a church fellowship

"Your kingdom come" is the best prayer to pray for any church. This is how Paul prayed for the Ephesian church.

Ephesians 1:15-19	Prayer topics & points to note
Verse 15: "For this reason, ever since I heard about your faith in the Lord Jesus and your love for all the saints,	1. People becoming Christians 2. Their love for fellow Christians
Verse 16: I have not stopped giving thanks for you, remembering you in prayers.	3. Paul's constant praying and the emphasis on giving thanks.
Verse 17: I keep asking that the God of our Lord Jesus Christ, the glorious Father, may give you the Spirit of wisdom and revelation, so that you may know him better.	4. The Spirit of wisdom 5. The Spirit of revelation 6. To know Jesus better
Verse 18: I pray also that the eyes of your heart may be enlightened in order that you may know the hope to which he has called you, the riches of his glorious inheritance in the saints,	7. Inner enlightenment 8. To know our future hope 9. To enjoy God's inheritance
Verse 19: and his incomparably great power for us who believe.	10. To know God's great power

3. In our own lives

There is little point in praying for God's kingdom to be strengthened everywhere in the world if we do not want God to be King in our own lives.

The prayer we need to pray for ourselves should be along the lines of Paul's advice to the Christians at Rome.

"Therefore, I urge you, brothers, in view of God's mercy, to offer your bodies as living sacrifices, holy and pleasing to God – this is your spiritual act of worship." *Romans 12:1*

Your will be done on earth as it is in heaven

The place of God's will in our lives

1. God's will is to have priority over our will	"Yet not as I will, but as you will... May your will be done."	*Matthew 26:39,42*
2. Jesus' overriding desire was to do God's will.	"'My food'", said Jesus, 'is to do the will of him who sent me.'"	*John 4:34*
3. We are expected to find out what God's will is.	"Find out what pleases the Lord ... understand what the Lord's will is."	*Ephesians 5:10,17*

Praying "your will be done" for your own life

Paul reminded the Christians at Rome that God's will would only be carried out in their lives if they submitted their minds to God's will and God's renewal.

A SAYING ABOUT
PRAYER

IF YOU ARE TOO BUSY TO PRAY,
THEN YOU ARE TOO BUSY.

> "Do not be conformed to this world, but be transformed by the renewing of your minds, so that you may discern what is the will of God –
> what is good
>   and acceptable
>   and perfect."
> *Romans 12:2*

A PRAYER TO
PRAY

O LORD, MAKE YOUR WAY PLAIN
BEFORE ME.
LET YOUR GLORY BE MY END,
   YOUR WORD MY RULE,
      AND THEN YOUR WILL BE DONE.
AMEN.
King Charles I (1600-1649)

Praying for God's will

Pray for God's will to be done
   in your family
   in your church
   in your relationships
   in your city
   in your nation
   and in the world.

Give us today our daily bread

A prayer of dependence

When we pray, "Give us today our daily bread," we are expressing our dependence on God for all our needs, both spiritual and material.

A good daily prayer comes in Proverbs:

> "Keep falsehood and lies far from me; give me neither poverty or riches, but give me only my daily bread." *Proverbs 30:8*

A prayer for daily needs

It is a natural human reaction to difficulties to be anxious about not having what we need. This part of the Lord's prayer stresses "prayer and supplication with thanksgiving," as the Christian reaction to trouble.

> "Do not be anxious about anything, but by prayer and supplication with thanksgiving let your requests be made known to God, and the peace of God, which surpasses all understanding, will guard your hearts and your minds in Christ Jesus." *Philippians 4:6-7*

Daily bread and daily worry

The question is: If we believe that God is our loving heavenly Father, why do we worry so much?

Look at the birds

"Therefore I tell you, do not worry about your life, what you will eat or drink; or about your body, what you will wear. Is not life more important than food, and the body more important than clothes? Look at the birds of the air; they do not sow or reap or store away in barns, and yet your heavenly Father feeds them. Are you not much more valuable than they? Who of you by worrying can add a single hour to his life?" *Matthew 6:25-27*

Give *us* our daily bread

We find it easier to pray for our own daily needs than for those of the hungry and starving. Now that we live in a global village and know the plight of needy people in many different parts of the world, we can see very clearly that this part of the Lord's Prayer should extend to the whole world.

A seemingly kind word, but no action

James warned his readers about the gap between kind ideas and positive action for the needy.

> "Suppose a brother or sister is without clothes and daily food. If one of you says to him, 'Go, I wish you well; keep warm and well fed,' but does nothing about his physical needs, what good is it?"
> *James 2:15-16*

Forgive us ...
as we also have forgiven

No automatic forgiveness

The is the only part of the Lord's Prayer which Jesus immediately went on to explain.

> "For if you forgive men when they sin against you, your heavenly Father will also forgive you. But if you do not forgive men their sins, your Father will not forgive your sins." *Matthew 6:14-15*

Forgive others

We have our sins forgiven by our loving heavenly Father. He expects us to be kind and forgiving towards others.

> "Be kind and compassionate to one another, forgiving each other, just as in Christ God forgave you." *Ephesians 4:32*

Removing the sin barrier

For some people, forgiving other people seems an impossible height to climb and God's special help needs to be asked.

Holding a grudge against someone is a sin. Any unconfessed sin and any sin we don't want to root out from our lives has a very serious consequence on our praying.

> "But your iniquities have separated you from your God; your sins have hidden his face from you, so that he will not hear you." *Isaiah 59:2*

Time for a spiritual check up

Praying this part of the Lord's Prayer gives you an opportunity to give yourself a spiritual check up.

• **Ask the Holy Spirit to show you your sins.**
Pray this prayer from the psalms.

"Search me, O God, and know my heart; test me and know my anxious thoughts. See if there is any offensive way in me, and lead me in the way everlasting."
Psalm 139:23-24

• **Confess your sins to God, being as specific as possible.**
Recall this proverb.

"He who conceals his sins does not prosper, but whoever confesses and renounces them finds mercy."
Proverbs 28:13

• **Make restitution or amends as necessary.**
What did Jesus say on this subject? Jesus said we are to put things right with other people before we worship him.

"Therefore, if you are offering your gift at the altar and there remember that your brother has something against you, leave your gift there in front of the altar. First go and be reconciled to your brother; then come and offer your gift." *Matthew 5:23-24*

41

A PRAYER TO
PRAY

FATHER, SEEING HOW FREELY YOU HAVE LOVED ME WITH MY IMPERFECTIONS, GRANT THAT I MAY EQUALLY LOVE OTHERS WITH THEIRS. AMEN.
Author unknown

Lead us not into temptation

Being tempted is no sin in itself

Jesus was himself tempted on many occasions. It is giving way to temptation that is sinful.

> "Then Jesus was led by the Spirit into the desert to be tempted by the devil." *Matthew 4:1*

An analysis of temptation

1 Corinthians 10:13	Lessons to learn
"No temptation has seized you except what is common to man."	1. Everyone is tempted. Yes everyone from the Christian you admire the most, down to yourself. No one escapes temptation.
"And God is faithful."	2. God is not letting us down by allowing a temptation to attack us. He promises to stay at our side through it.
"He will not let you be tempted beyond what you can bear."	3. God knows our limits. He promises that we will never be tempted beyond the power he gives us.
"But when you are tempted, he will also provide a way out so that you can stand up under it."	4. We need to turn to God in prayer before, during and after temptation. He promises to help us and to provide a way out of temptation so we must go to him for this supernatural assistance.

Overcoming temptation

Some Christians claim that, in answer to prayer, God has instantly and miraculously delivered them from a particular temptation. But the experience of most Christians is that the battle against temptation is life-long. God has provided a number of spiritual weapons for Christians to use in this spiritual warfare.

• The Bible

When faced with temptation, Jesus quoted the Bible against the Tempter. *See Matthew 4:4, 7, 11*

Using memorized Bible verses can be a great help when you are being tempted.

"I have hidden your word in my heart that I might not sin against you." *Psalm 119:11*

• Humility

It is when we think that we are doing fine and won't fall under temptation that we are most at risk of falling.

"So, if you think you are standing firm, be careful that you don't fall!" *1 Corinthians 10:12*

• Watchfulness and prayerfulness

At one of the most critical moments in Jesus' life (in the Garden of Gethsemane) Jesus told his disciples to watch and pray.

"*Watch and pray* so that you will not fall into temptation." *Matthew 26:41*

Recording the same event Luke writes that Jesus said: "Pray so that you will not fall into temptation." *Luke 22:40*

Deliver us from the evil one

The devil tempts, God tests

The devil tempts us in order to knock us down; God tests us in order to build us up.

> "When tempted, no one should say, 'God is tempting me.' For God cannot be tempted by evil, nor does he tempt anyone." *James 1:13*

A spiritual battle

Followers of Jesus face a spiritual battle every day. Satan wants to defeat us through temptation. So we pray for God's protection as we pray the Lord's Prayer.

Francis of Assisi

Francis of Assisi suggested that we should pray the following prayer when we come to this part of the Lord's Prayer.

> "Protect us from past evil.
> Protect us from present evil.
> Free us from future evil."

Handy hint from James

James told his readers how to defeat the devil. We do what he says as we pray this last part of the Lord's Prayer.

> "Submit yourselves, then, to God. Resist the devil, and he will flee from you." *James 4:7*

The kingdom, the power, and the glory

At the end of the Lord's Prayer we often pray what is known as the doxology, "For yours is the kingdom, and the power and the glory, for ever and ever. Amen."

These words may have been added by a scribe and may not have been given by Jesus in his original prayer. Yet they are suitable words to round off the Lord Prayer as the words – kingdom, power and glory – are strongly featured in the Bible.

• God's power
"Be strong in the Lord and in his mighty power."
Ephesians 6:10

• God's kingdom
"All you have made will praise you, O Lord; your saints will extol you. They will tell of the glory of your kingdom and speak of your might, so that all men may know of your mighty acts and the glorious splendor of your kingdom. Your kingdom is an everlasting kingdom, and your dominion endures through all generations."
Psalm 145:10-13

• God's glory
"Yours, O Lord, is the greatness and the power and the glory and the majesty and the splendor, for everything in heaven and earth is yours. Yours, O Lord, is the kingdom; you are exalted as head over all." *1 Chronicles 29:11*

Psalms for times of crisis

Prayer book and hymn book
In Old Testament times the Psalms were the prayer book and hymn book of God's people. Jews and Christians alike have drawn strength from them.

The one hundred and fifty psalms cover a wide variety of themes and it is helpful to know which psalms suit our particular needs.

Psalms in a time of crisis
1. Choose a psalm to read.
2. Read it all the way through.
3. Ask God to comfort you through its words.
4. Read it again, verse by verse. Pause and reflect on each verse before moving on to the next one.

Psalm 23
Psalm 23 has been called the Shepherd's Psalm. But the shepherd does not speak at all. So it has also been called the Sheep's Psalm, for the sheep do all the speaking.

The Lord is my shepherd, I shall not be in want.
He makes me lie down in green pastures,
he leads me beside quiet waters,
    he restores my soul.
He guides me in paths of righteousness
    for his name's sake.
Even though I walk
    through the valley of the shadow of death,
I will fear no evil,
    for you are with me;
your rod and your staff,
    they comfort me.
Your prepare a table before me
    in the presence of my enemies.
You anoint my head with oil;
    my cup overflows.
Surely goodness and love will follow me
    all the days of my life,
and I will dwell in the house of the Lord
    for ever.
Psalm 23:1-6

You prepare a table before me

This "table" was essential to wounded or sick sheep.

Healthy sheep did not care for ill sheep. At best, they would go over to the sick sheep and eat all the grass around him, leaving him none. At worst, they would butt him and push him around. So the shepherd prepared a "table" for the sick sheep.

The shepherd marked out an area about 20 ft (7 meters) x 15 ft (5 meters). He put his rod on one side and his staff on the other side. He lay down at the top of the protective rectangle, after he had placed his cloak at the bottom. No other sheep dared to cross over the rod, staff, cloak or shepherd to eat any of the grass.

In the presence of his enemies the ill sheep now had a "table" to protect him.

Psalms to turn to in a time of crisis

Psalms 4; 5; 11; 28; 41; 55; 59; 64; 70; 109; 120; 140; 141; 142.

Psalms for times of joy

Joy in the Psalms

Over the next month, select one verse about joy from the Psalms and take it with you through your day.

1. Joy and the heart	"You have filled my heart with greater joy ..." *(See also Psalms 19:8; 28:7; 97:11; 119:111.)*	*Psalm 4:7*
2. Joy and shouting and singing praises	"Let them ever sing for joy." *(See also Psalms 20:5; 27:6; 33:3; 35:27; 42:4; 47:1, 5; 65:8, 13; 66:1; 67:4; 71:23; 81:1; 89:12; 92:4; 95:1; 96:12; 98:4, 6, 8; 10:43; 107:22; 118:15; 126:2, 5, 6; 132:9, 16; 137:3; 149:5.)*	*Psalm 5:11.*
3. Joy in God's presence	"You will fill me with joy in your presence." *(See also Psalm 21:6.)*	*Psalm 16:11*
4. Joy linked to delight and gladness	"... to God, my joy and my delight." *(See also Psalms 45:15; 51:8; 90:14.)*	*Psalm 43:4*
5. Filled with joy	"We are filled with joy."	*Psalm 126:3*
6. Joy and salvation	"Restore to me the joy of your salvation."	*Psalm 51:12*
7. Clothed with joy	"... clothed me with joy."	*Psalm 30:11*
8. Anointed with joy	"God, your God, has set you above your companions by anointing you with the oil of joy."	*Psalm 45:7*
9. Comfort and joy	"When anxiety was great within me, your consolation brought joy to my soul."	*Psalm 94:19*

Psalm 100

Shout for joy to the Lord, all the earth.
Worship the Lord with gladness;
   come before him with joyful songs.
Know that the Lord is God.
   It is he who made us, and we are his;
   we are his people, the sheep of his
   pasture.
Enter his gates with thanksgiving
   and his courts with praise;
   give thanks to him and praise his name.
For the Lord is good and his love endures
   for ever;
   his faithfulness continues through all
   generations.
Psalm 100:1-5

Hallelujah Psalms

These psalms use the term Hallelujah,
meaning "Praise Jah (Jehovah)".
   *Psalms 115; 116; 117; 146; 147; 148;
149; 150.*

A PRAYER TO
PRAY

LORD, MAKE ME AN INSTRUMENT OF YOUR PEACE.
WHERE THERE IS HATRED, LET ME SOW LOVE,
WHERE THERE IS INJURY, PARDON,
WHERE THERE IS DOUBT, FAITH,
WHERE THERE IS DARKNESS, LIGHT,
WHERE THERE IS SADNESS, JOY.

O DIVINE MASTER, GRANT THAT I MAY NOT SO MUCH
    SEEK TO BE CONSOLED AS TO CONSOLE,
NOT SO MUCH TO BE UNDERSTOOD AS TO
UNDERSTAND,
NOT SO MUCH TO BE LOVED AS TO LOVE;
FOR IT IS IN GIVING THAT WE RECEIVE,
IT IS IN PARDONING THAT WE ARE PARDONED,
IT IS IN DYING THAT WE ARE BORN TO ETERNAL LIFE.

Traditionally attributed to Francis of Assisi

Psalms for times of dryness

Spiritual dryness and the Christian

It is true that unconfessed sin can and does cause much disturbance in a Christian's walk with Jesus.

A SAYING ABOUT PRAYER

"SEVEN DAYS WITHOUT PRAYER MAKES ONE WEAK."

> "If I had cherished sin in my heart, the Lord would not have listened [to my prayers]." *Psalm 66:18*

It is not true that all spiritual dryness can be put down to unconfessed sin.

Psalms 42 and 43

When you are down, read Psalms 42 and 43.

Write down in a notebook what lessons God teaches you as you read slowly through them for a second time.

Lessons from Psalms 42 and 43

Lesson number one: Tell God what you feel like

1. The Psalmist admitted his own feelings. He talks about being "downcast" in *Psalm 42:5-6, 11; 43:5*	"My soul is downcast within me." *Psalm 42:5*
2. The Psalmist does not beat about the bush. He describes specific troubles and symptoms. Godly people can easily feel low when attacked by unbelievers.	"My bones suffer mortal agony as my foes taunt me, saying to me all day long, 'Where is your God?'" *Psalm 42:10*
3. The Psalmist tells God that he feels that the Lord has forsaken and forgotten him.	"Why have you forgotten me?" *Psalm 42:9* "Why have you rejected me?" *Psalm 43:2*

Lesson number two: Remember who God is

1. The Psalmist calls God his Rock.	"I say to God my Rock." *Psalm 42:9*
2. God can give the Psalmist light and truth.	"Send forth your light and your truth, let them guide me." *Psalm 43:3*
3. The Psalmist remembers that God is his stronghold.	"You God are my stronghold." *Psalm 43:2*
4. God is the Psalmist's Savior.	"... my Savior and my God." *Psalm 42:11; 43:5*

Lesson number three: Put your trust in God

The Psalmist gives himself a good talking to and concludes that he must trust God.	"Put your hope in God, for I will yet praise him, my Savior and my God." *Psalm 42:11; 43:5*

Psalms for times of sin

Psalm 51

This psalm is thought to have been written after David had committed adultery with Bathsheba, and in an attempt to cover this up arranged for Bathsheba's husband, Uriah, to be killed in battle. *See 2 Samuel 11.*

How could an adulterer and murderer continue to serve God? Only because he prayed Psalm 51 from his heart.

Read through the psalm for yourself and see how each verse has a positive message for a repentant sinner.

Have mercy on me, O God

Verse

1 Have mercy on me, O God, according to your unfailing love; according to your great compassion blot out my transgressions.

2 Wash away all my iniquity and cleanse me from my sin.

3 For I know my transgressions, and my sin is always before me.

4 Against you, you only, have I sinned and done what is evil in your sight, so that you are proved right when you speak and justified when you judge.

5 Surely I was sinful at birth, sinful from the time my mother conceived me.

6 Surely you desire truth in the inner parts; you teach me wisdom in the inmost place.

7 Cleanse me with hyssop, and I will be clean; wash me, and I will be whiter than snow.

8 Let me hear joy and gladness; let the bones you have crushed rejoice.

9 Hide your face from my sins and blot out all my iniquity.

10 Create in me a pure heart, O God, and renew a steadfast spirit within me.

11 Do not cast me from your presence or take your Holy Spirit from me.

12 Restore to me the joy of your salvation and grant me a willing spirit, to sustain me.

13 Then I will teach transgressors your ways, and sinners will turn back to you.

14 Save me from bloodguilt, O God, the God who saves me, and my tongue will sing of your righteousness.

15 O Lord, open my lips, and my mouth will declare your praise.

16 You do not delight in sacrifice, or I would bring it; you do not take pleasure in burnt offerings.

17 The sacrifices of God are a broken spirit; a broken and contrite heart, O God, you will not despise.

18 In your good pleasure make Zion prosper; build up the walls of Jerusalem.

19 Then there will be righteous sacrifices, whole burnt offerings to delight you; then bulls will be offered on your altar.

Psalm 51

What kind of prayers does God answer?
Prayers that come from:

1. An obedient heart	"… we receive from him [God] anything we ask, because we obey his commands."	*1 John 3:22*
2. A forgiving heart	"And when you stand praying, if you hold anything against anyone, forgive him, so that your Father in heaven may forgive you your sins."	*Mark 11:25*
3. A heart that does not doubt	"But when he asks, he must believe and not doubt, because he who doubts is like a wave of the sea, blown and tossed by the wind."	*James 1:6*
4. A broken heart	"A broken and contrite heart, O God, you will not despise."	*Psalm 51:17*
5. An undivided heart	"You will seek me and find me when you seek me with all your heart."	*Jeremiah 29:13*
6. A prayerful heart	"If you remain in me and my words remain in you, ask whatever you wish, and it will be given you."	*John 15:7*
7. A heart taught by	"The Spirit helps us in our weakness. We do not know what we ought to pray for, but the Spirit himself intercedes for us with groans that words cannot express."	*Romans 8:26*

53

Psalms
Psalms which breathe deep sorrow for sin:
Psalms 6; 25; 32; 38; 39; 40; 51; 102; 130.

Jesus at prayer

Jesus often prayed

"Jesus *often* withdrew to lonely places and prayed." *Luke 5:16*

Matthew, Mark, Luke and John record fifteen occasions when Jesus prayed. The writer to the Hebrews adds,

> "During the days of Jesus' life on earth, he offered up prayers and petitions with loud cries and tears to the one who could save him from death, and he was heard because of his reverent submission." *Hebrews 5:7*

Jesus is our model

There are many ways in which we can imitate Jesus in his praying.

1. Jesus praised God

"At that time Jesus, full of joy through the Holy Spirit, said, 'I praise you Father, Lord of heaven and earth, because you have hidden these things from the wise and learned, and revealed them to little children.'" *Luke 10:21*

2. Jesus gave thanks to God

Before feeding the 5,000, Jesus asked God to bless the five loaves and two fish.

"Taking the five loaves and the two fish and looking up to heaven, he gave thanks and broke the loaves." *Mark 6:41*

3. Jesus asked for things in his prayers

In his moment of great distress Jesus prayed to his heavenly Father.

"On reaching the place, he said to them, 'Pray that you will not fall into temptation.'

He withdrew about a stone's throw beyond them, knelt down and prayed, 'Father, if you are willing, take this cup from me; yet not my will, but yours be done.'

An angel from heaven appeared to him and strengthened him.

And being in anguish, he prayed more earnestly, and his sweat was like drops of blood falling to the ground." *Luke 22:40-44*

4. Jesus prayed for other people

"When they came to the place of the Skull, there they crucified him, along with the criminals – one on his right, the other on his left. Jesus said, 'Father, forgive them, for they do not know what they are doing.'" *Luke 23:34*

54

Jesus prayed at critical times in his life

1. At his baptism

"When all the people were being baptized, Jesus was baptized too. And as he was praying, heaven was opened and the Holy Spirit descended on him in bodily form like a dove." *Luke 3:21-22*

2. Before he chose his twelve disciples

"One of those days Jesus went out to a mountainside to pray, and spent the night praying to God. When morning came, he called his disciples to him and chose twelve of them." *Luke 6:13*

3. In face of temptation

After the miracle of the feeding of the five thousand the people tried to make Jesus their king. This was a temptation to avoid the cross and Jesus overcame this temptation by seeking refuge in prayer.

"After the people saw the miraculous sign that Jesus did, they began to say, 'Surely this is the Prophet who is to come into the world.' Jesus, knowing that they intended to come and make him king by force, withdrew again to a mountain by himself." *John 6:14-15*

4. From the cross

"Jesus called out with a loud voice, 'Father, into your hands I commit my spirit.'" *Luke 23:46*

"Jesus said, 'It is finished.' With that he bowed his head and gave up his spirit." *John 19:30*

55

Praying for others

The prophet Samuel and prayer

Prayer dominated Samuel's life, from start to finish.

1. He was born in answer to prayer.	*See 1 Samuel 1:10-28*
2. His name means *asked of God.*	*See 1 Samuel 1:20*
3. Deliverance at Mispah came	*See 1 Samuel 7:2-13*
4. When Israel asked for a king, Samuel prayed.	*See 1 Samuel 8:6, 21*
5. He prayed for his people all the time.	"As for me, far be it from me that I should sin against the Lord by failing to pray for you." *1 Samuel 12:23*

Samuel thought that it was sinful not to pray for God's people.

What about keeping a prayer list?

On one page you could have *Prayers for Every Day.* This might include your closest family and friends.

The next seven pages could be for each day of the week. By adding people's names and things to pray for on these days it would ensure that you pray for them once a week.

You could also use the next thirty-one pages to pray for different people and things once a month.

Is it wrong or selfish to bother God with trifling things?

Parents long for their children to tell them about all the joys and difficulties of their days. And God loves us much more than any parent can.

"... in everything, by prayer and petition with thanksgiving, present your requests to God." *Philippians 4:6*

Praying for your friends, children and spiritual children

What should you pray for when you pray for your friends? Christians are spiritual parents to those they lead to Christ and to those they are spiritually responsible for. They will pray for the same things that Christian parents pray for their children.

1. That they will know Jesus as their Savior.

2. That they will be protected from Satan in all areas of their lives: spiritual, emotional and physical. Pray as Jesus did. "My prayer is not that you will take them out of the world but that you protect them from the evil one." *John 17:15*

3. That they will have good friends, desire the right kind of friends and be protected from the wrong kind of friends. "My son, if sinners entice you, do not give in to them. If they say 'Come along with us; let's lie in wait for someone's blood, let's waylay some harmless soul.'" *Proverbs 1:10-11*

4. That they will serve Jesus Christ wholeheartedly. "Therefore, I urge you, brothers, in view of God's mercy, to offer your bodies as living sacrifices, holy and pleasing to God – which is your spiritual worship. Do not conform any longer to the pattern of this world, but be transformed by the renewing of your mind. Then you will be able to test and approve what God's will is – his good, pleasing and perfect will." *Romans 12:1-2*

When we pray are we asking God to change his mind?

There are many things about prayer that are a mystery. But it seems that God, in his love, calls us to be his partners in his work in this world.

"For we are God's fellow-workers." *1 Corinthians 3:9*

Jesus commands us to pray. *See Luke 10:2*
We are promised that our prayers are effective. *See James 5:16*

Keeping a prayer diary

A prayer diary of journal
This is different from a prayer list which is just a list of people and things to pray for.

A prayer diary is a record of how you have found that God has answered your prayers. By recording how God has answered a request, you will be encouraged to keep praying.

Making a prayer diary
In a notebook draw four columns down the page.

Column 1	Column 2	Column 3	Column 4
Date of prayer request	Prayer request	How prayer was answered	Date of answered prayer

Then fill in a line with the details of the most important thing you are praying about this week.

You can add to it as much as you like. One topic per week is manageable for most people.

When a prayer request is answered that is the cue for giving thanks to God.

Praying for people to be converted

"I spent the evening praying incessantly for divine assistance and that I might not be self-dependent. What I passed through was remarkable, and there appeared to be nothing of any importance to me but holiness of heart and life, and the conversion of the heathen to God. I cared not where or how I lived, or what hardships I went through so that I could but gain souls to Christ."
David Brainerd, Diary, 21 July 1744

So why does so much prayer seem to be unanswered?

We have such wonderful promises about prayer in the Bible from Jesus.

"If you believe, you will receive whatever you ask for in prayer."
Matthew 21:22

1. Being out of tune with God and His word	"If you remain in me and my words remain in you, ask whatever you wish, and it will be given you."	*John 15:7*
2. Lack of desire to please Jesus	"We ... receive from him anything we ask, because we obey his commands and do what pleases him."	*1 John 3:22*
3. Unconfessed sin	"The face of the Lord is against those who do evil."	*1 Peter 3:12*
4. Having the wrong motives	"When you ask, you do not receive, because you ask with wrong motives, that you may spend what you get on your pleasures."	*James 4:3*
5. Praying with lack of faith	"Without faith it is impossible to please God."	*Hebrews 11:6*
6. Lack of perseverance	"Then Jesus told his disciples a parable to show them that they should always pray and not give up."	*Luke 18:1*

Paul's prayers

Paul's prayers for the first Christian churches

Paul's thirteen letters in the New Testament were not just filled with giving instructions but they record the prayers he prayed for the different churches.

Paul's prayer for the Ephesians

"For this reason I kneel before the Father, from whom his whole family in heaven and on earth derives its name. I pray that out of his glorious riches he may strengthen you with power through his Spirit in your inner being, so that Christ may dwell in your hearts through faith. And I pray that you, being rooted and established in love, may have power, together with all the saints, to grasp how wideand long and high and deep is the love of Christ, and to know this love that surpasses knowledge – that you may be filled to the measure of all the fullness of God."
Ephesians 3:14-19

Church written to
1. The Ephesians
2. The Philippians
3. The Colossians
4. The Thessalonians

60

Pray Bible prayers

One way to pray for people is to select a prayer in the Bible, such as Ephesians 3:14-19, and use it as a basis of prayer, praying the prayer that Paul prayed for the Ephesian Christians – inserting the name of someone you are concerned for today.

Romans 16

Paul prayed for people by name. Have you ever read through Romans 16 and thought it consisted of just a long list of names? Read through this list of over two dozen people and see what Paul prayed for as he mentioned each person by name.

Theme of prayer	Extract from prayer	
Enlightenment	"That you may know the hope to which he has called you."	*Ephesians 1:18 (See Ephesians 1:15-19)*
Perseverence	"He who began a good work in you will carry it on to completion until the day of Christ Jesus."	*Philippians 1:6*
God's will	"... asking God to fill you with the knowledge of his will through all spiritual wisdom and understanding."	*Colossians 1:9*
Thanksgiving for faith, love, and hope	"We continually remember before our God and Father your work produced by faith, your labor prompted by love, and your endurance inspired by hope in our Lord Jesus Christ."	*1 Thessalonians 1:2-3*

Should you pray for people you've never seen?

Here is Paul's prayer for a group of Christians he had never met.

"Since the day we heard about you, we have not stopped praying for you and asking God to fill you with the knowledge of his will."
Colossians 1:9

More Bible prayers

How James said we should pray
James 5:13-18

Verse

14 "Is any one of you sick? He should call the elders of the church to pray over him and anoint him with oil in the name of the Lord."

15 "And the prayer offered in faith will make the sick person well; the Lord will raise him up. If he has sinned, he will be forgiven."

16 "Therefore confess your sins to each other and pray for each other so that you may be healed. The prayer of a righteous man is powerful and effective."

17 "Elijah was a man just like us. He prayed earnestly that it would not rain, and it did not rain on the land for three and a half years."

1. Be united in prayer.	"Call the elders of the church to pray."	*Verse 14*
2. Believe as you pray.	"The prayer offered in faith."	*Verse 15*
3. Have your own sin dealt with before you pray.	"Confess your sins to each other."	*Verse 16*
4. Pray for others.	"Pray for each other."	*Verse 16*
5. Be definite as you pray.	"That it would not rain."	*Verse 17*

Making progress in prayer

One of the best ways to find help in praying is to turn to the prayers in the Bible and see what God teaches you about how other people prayed to God.

King Hezekiah's song of praise for healing

"A writing of Hezekiah king of Judah after his illness and recovery:

I said, 'In the prime of my life
    must I go through the gates of death
    and be robbed of the rest of my years?'
I said, 'I will not again see the Lord,
    the Lord, in the land of the living;
no longer will I look on mankind,
    or be with those who now dwell in this world.
... But what can I say?
    He has spoken to me, and he himself has done this.
I will walk humbly all my years
    because of this anguish of my soul.
Lord, by such things men live;
    and my spirit finds life in them too.
You restored me to health
    and let me live. ...
The living, the living – they praise you,
    as I am doing today;
fathers tell their children
    about your faithfulness.
Isaiah 38:9-11, 15-16, 19

Praising God
despite everything

Pray anyway

There are no times when we should not pray. But different kinds of prayers are appropriate to different situations.

IF ANYONE WOULD TELL YOU THE SHORTEST WAY TO ALL HAPPINESS AND ALL PERFECTION, HE MUST TELL YOU TO MAKE IT A RULE TO YOURSELF TO THANK AND PRAISE GOD FOR EVERYTHING THAT HAPPENS TO YOU.
FOR IT IS CERTAIN THAT WHATEVER CALAMITY HAPPENS TO YOU, IF YOU THANK AND PRAISE GOD FOR IT, YOU TURN IT INTO A BLESSING.
William Law

"Is any one of you in trouble? He should pray. Is anyone happy? Let him sing songs of praise."
James 5:13

God's promised presence

"The Lord our God is near us whenever we pray to him."
Deuteronomy 4:7

64

So God is close to us when we pray, whether we feel him or not; whether we are on our own or with many other people. This is good to remember when we just don't feel like praying.

Disasters and prayer

The fall of Jerusalem and the destruction of the temple was the greatest disaster the Israelites suffered. Yet these words of hope and burning faith are found in the middle of the Book of Lamentations, a book which describes their devastating condition.

"Because of the Lord's great love we
    are not consumed,
  for his compassions never fail.
They are new every morning,
    great is your faithfulness."
Lamentations 3:22-23

Daily
Devotions
made easy

Despite the importance of daily devotions, time alone with God is often the first casualty in the war for our time. Work, advertisements, chores, family duties, and the endless stream of computerized and televised entertainment all fight to maintain their hold on our daily life.

Our own struggle for sanity in the face of distraction often leaves us defensive, isolated, and alienated from God and our neighbours.

Christians throughout the centuries have expressed their devotion to God and each other by setting aside times in the day as sacred, and by expressing their love of God in the ordinary and mundane moments as well.

Daily Devotions made easy provides concrete examples of ways that Christians have created lifestyles which incline their hearts toward the Kingdom throughout their busy lives.

Contents

The example of Jesus

Jesus prayed on his own
"Very early in the morning, while it was still dark, Jesus got up, left the house and went off to a solitary place, where he prayed." *Mark 1:35*

Jesus prayed with others
"He went to Nazareth, where he had been brought up, and on the Sabbath day he went into the synagogue, as was his custom." *Luke 4:16*

Jesus prayed when under extreme pressure
[In the garden of Gethsemane Jesus prayed:] "'Father, if you are willing, take this cup from me; yet not my will, but yours be done.'" *Luke 22:42*

Jesus sometimes prayed all night long
"Jesus . . . spent the night praying to God." *Luke 6:12*

Jesus prayed as he died
"Jesus called out with a loud voice, 'Father, into your hands I commit my spirit.' When he had said this, he breathed his last." *Luke 23:46*

With others

Acts 2:42

"They devoted themselves to the apostles' teaching and to the fellowship, to the breaking of bread and to prayer." *Acts 2:42*

At least thirty-five times in the Acts of the Apostles, Luke mentions that the early followers of Jesus prayed. And in most of these instances they were praying with each other. Perhaps one of the greatest differences between the first century church and the church today is their practice of praying together.

Praying together in the Acts of the Apostles

Read through Acts and note where prayer or worship is mentioned. Then see if the reference is to an individual praying on his or her own or a group of Christians praying together.

Acts 1:14	"They all joined together constantly in prayer, along with the women and Mary the mother of Jesus, and with his brothers."
Acts 2:46-47	"Every day they continued to meet together in the temple courts. They broke bread in their homes and ate together with glad and sincere hearts, praising God . . ."
Acts 3:1	"One day Peter and John were going up to the temple at the time of prayer – at three in the afternoon."
Acts 4:23-24	"On their release, Peter and John went back to their own people and reported all that the chief priests and elders had said to them. When they heard this, they raised their voices together in prayer to God."
Acts 5:12	"The apostles performed many miraculous signs and wonders among the people. And all the believers used to meet together in Solomon's Colonnade."
Acts 6:4	"We will . . . give our attention to prayer and the ministry of the word."
Acts 12:12	"When this had dawned on him [Peter], he went to the house of Mary the mother of John, also called Mark, where many people had gathered and were praying."
Acts 16:16	"Once when *we* were going to the place of prayer, we were met by a slave girl who had a spirit . . ."

No solitary religion
It's been said that "The New Testament knows nothing of solitary religion."

A command from Hebrews
"Let us not give up meeting together, as some are in the habit of doing, but let us encourage one another – and all the more as you see the Day approaching." *Hebrews 10:25*

John Wesley's secret: societies
Many have wondered why so many people who were touched by the Methodist revival in England led by John Wesley grew into strong Christians. Wesley himself wrote:

> "Our *societies* were formed from those who were wandering upon the dark mountains, that belonged to no Christian church; but were awakened by the preaching of the Methodists who set up the standard of the cross in the streets of the cities, in the lanes of the villages, in the barns, and farmer's kitchens."

Every convert had to belong to a local *society* and attend a weekly meeting for group prayer and mutual Christian support and fellowship.

On your own

It's not "either . . . or", but, "both . . . and"

It's not a question of: Should I meet up with other Christians to pray, or should I pray on my own? Rather it's a logical inference that I should both worship with Christians *and* pray on my own.

People who valued daily devotions

- John Wesley regularly got up to pray and read the Bible at 4 A.M.
- Luther used to say, "I am going to be so busy today, I have to spend not one hour, but two hours in prayer, before I can do anything else."
- Since he was converted at the age of sixteen, Billy Graham has made it his aim to set aside a time for prayer and Bible reading at the start and end of every day.

- Robert Murray M'Cheyne, 1813-43, the godly Scottish pastor, used to say, "I ought to spend the best hours in communion with God. It is my noblest and most fruitful employment, and is not to be thrust into a corner. The morning hours, from six to eight, are the most uninterrupted and should thus be employed."

8

The example of Daniel

"Now when Daniel learned that the decree had been published [which said he would be thrown to the lions if he prayed to God], he went home to his upstairs room where the windows opened towards Jerusalem. Three times a day he got down on his knees and prayed, giving thanks to his God, just as he had done before." *Daniel 6:10*

Speaking

When you are on your own praying, start with worship. Many Christians confess their sins to God, ask God for things, and remember to thank God for answered prayer . . . but they are weak on worshiping God.

The psalms are full of worship

"Come, let us bow down in worship,
    let us kneel before the LORD our Maker;
for he is our God
    and we are the people of his pasture,
    the flock of his care."
Psalm 95:6-7

Listening

The main way we listen to God is when we read the Bible. God speaks to us in his Word. It is all too easy to read a passage of the Bible without asking prayerfully for God to speak to our hearts through it. We should approach our daily reading of the Bible with humble hearts as well as keen minds.

Bible Reading Schedules

There are many different types of Bible reading devotional schedules available which will give you a manageable passage of the Bible to read each day, along with helpful comments. If you have been using a schedule like this for a year or so, consider the possibility of moving on to another type of devotional reading schedule or some other form of Bible study that will stretch you even more.

> **The Bible in your life and thoughts**
> "The vigor of our spiritual life will be in exact proportion to the place held by the Bible in our life and thoughts."
> *George Müller*

"I missed my prayer time."

If you seem to oversleep and have no time to pray and read the Bible, use this book as an impetus to begin daily devotions.

If you have skipped praying and reading the Bible, not just for the odd day or week, but for months and months, again, use this book as an impetus to begin daily devotions.

Ask God to help you. Tell him that you are genuinely sorry about your lackadaisical attitude toward a quiet time with him.

Five conditions for prevailing prayer

George Müller, the German-born Christian philanthropist, continually asked God to provide milk and bread for his numerous orphanages in Bristol, England. Müller never asked for money from people, he just prayed for it. He kept the following five conditions of prevailing prayer in his mind:

1. Entire dependence upon the merits and intercession of the Lord Jesus Christ, as the only basis for any request for blessing.
2. Separation from all known sin.
3. Faith in God's word of promise.
4. Asking in agreement with his will.
5. A refusal to give up. There must be *waiting on* God and *waiting for* God.

Have a plan (part 1)

I've never done this before

Here is a seven-point plan to get you going. You can start by following it and then adapt it to suit your own needs.

How much time should I spend?

Try ten minutes. It's better to start small and succeed, than to be overambitious and to feel that you failed everyday.

Do I stand, sit, kneel or what?

It does not actually matter. But kneeling down does show your dependence on God.

"All the disciples and their wives and children accompanied us out of the city, and there on the beach we knelt to pray."
Acts 21:5

The Lord's Prayer

When the disciples asked Jesus to teach them to pray, he gave them the Lord's Prayer. So, pray the Lord's Prayer

Our Father
who art in heaven,
hallowed be thy name;
thy kingdom come;
thy will be done;
on earth as it is in heaven.
Give us this day our daily bread.
And forgive us our trespasses,
as we forgive those who trespass
against us.
And lead us not into temptation;
but deliver us from evil.
For thine is the kingdom, the
power,
and the glory, for ever and ever.
Amen.

This is a traditional form of the Lord's Prayer, but you may prefer to use a more up to date form.

Pray the Lord's Prayer . . . again!

This time, go through the Lord's prayer, spending a few moments on each line.

For "Our Father" you may reflect on what a wonderful God you have and pray: "Thank you, heavenly Father, that you are such a wonderful God."

Then move on to the next line of the prayer, doing the same thing, until you reach the end of the prayer.

Read one chapter of the Bible

Try reading one chapter of Mark's Gospel one day, and then one psalm the next day.

Pray for others

Start with your family and those closest to you.

Pray for yourself

Go through your day in your mind, asking God to help you, especially in those troubling, tough times.

A poet's perspective

More things are wrought by prayer than this world dreams of:
For what are men better than sheep or goats
If, knowing God, they lift not hands of prayer
Both for themselves and those who call them friend.
Alfred Lloyd Tennyson

Have a plan (part 2)

How to start reading the Bible every day

If you've never tried Bible reading schedules, buy the ones which suit you best from a Christian bookstore.

Step one: pray

Before you open your Bible, pray.

A good prayer to pray just before you read your Bible is one based on Psalm 119:18:

"Open my eyes that I may see wonderful things in your law."

Step two: read the Bible passage

Many people who used Bible reading schedules never actually read the Bible! They just read the comments. Make sure you never do this. Start by reading the passage from the Bible suggested in the Bible reading schedule.

Step three: think

Remember, the Holy Spirit is your Teacher. Ask the Holy Spirit to help you. Ask yourself: What is the main point of the passage?

One of the best ways to understand any passage in the Bible is to ask these three further questions:

1. What does the passage teach about God: God the Father, God the Son or God the Holy Spirit?

Another way of doing this is to ask the question: If I knew nothing at all about God or about Jesus, what would this passage teach me?

2. Is there are command to obey, or a warning in the passage?

Bible reading is not just for your mind. It is meant to direct and mold your life. The instructions or the joys which you read in the Bible need to be put into practice in your life. So think about the problems you are facing at the moment. Ask God to show you how today's verses apply in detail.

3. Is there a promise to claim in the passage?

If you have just read the last verse in Matthew's Gospel, where Jesus says, "'I am with you always'" (Matthew 28:20), latch on to the promise. Think about your worries. How would this promise change your situation if you took it seriously? Then thank God for the promise and ask that you may trust him and that particular promise through the day.

Step four: Re-read the Bible passage

See if there is one thought, phrase, or word that shines out for you. Latch on to it and try and keep it with you all day long.

Step five: Read

Read the comments in your Bible reading schedule.

Step six: Pray

• Thank God for speaking to your heart through the Bible passage.
• Ask for his help to follow his teaching and keep close to him today.

Some people find it helpful to jot down in a notebook the main point that God has shown them from the passage.

Have a plan (part 3)

How to read the Bible in a year

Here's a simple plan which will take you through the whole Bible in a year.

Read approximately three chapters a day each month. In addition to that, read one chapter from the book of Proverbs, or one psalm, or section of a psalm, every day. (For example, just 8 verses a day when you reach Psalm 119.)

If you prefer to read just one chapter a day, as well as a psalm or a chapter from Proverbs, it will take you three years to read through all sixty-six Bible books.

"Your word is a lamp to my feet and a light to my path."
Psalm 119:105

Remember your aim

As you read the Bible, your aim is to know God and his ways of working in the world. As you read, ask God to help you understand the chapters.

A prayer

"Lord Jesus, make yourself to me
a living bright reality
more present; to faith's vision keen
than any outward object seen."
Hudson Taylor

Month 1	Matthew; Isaiah
Month 2	Acts; Jeremiah; Lamentations
Month 3	Genesis; Exodus
Month 4	Leviticus; Hebrews; Numbers
Month 5	Deuteronomy; Joshua; Judges; Ruth
Month 6	1 Samuel; 2 Samuel; Philippians; John
Month 7	1 Kings; 2 Kings; 1 Corinthians; 2 Corinthians; 1 Timothy; 2 Timothy; Titus;
Month 8	1 Chronicles; 2 Chronicles; Luke
Month 9	Ezra; Nehemiah; Esther; Romans; Mark; Ecclesiastes
Month 10	Ezekiel; Daniel; Revelation
Month 11	Hosea; Joel; Amos; Obadiah; Jonah; Micah; Nahum; Habakkuk; Zephaniah; Haggai; Zecahriah; Malachi; 1 Thessalonians; 2 Thessalonians
Month 12	Song of Songs; Job; Galatians; Ephesians; Colossians; Philemon; James; 1 Peter; 2 Peter; 1 John; 2 John; 3 John; Jude

Reading Scripture

"I began to read the holy Scriptures upon my knees, laying aside all other books, and praying over, if possible, every line and word. This proved meat indeed and drink indeed to my soul. I daily received fresh life, light and power from above." *George Whitefield, Journal*

What feeds the soul?

The Bible is like no other book

We talk of some books as being inspired. We say that Shakespeare or some of the Greek poets were inspired in their writings. But no other book in the world is inspired in the same way as the Bible is inspired.

The Bible is inspired by God and feeds our souls. The Bible writers themselves describe God's Word as bread, milk, solid food (or meat), and honey.

Not by bread alone

"'Man does not live by bread alone, but on every word that comes from the mouth of God.'"
Matthew 4:4

Milk to make you grow

"Like newborn babies, crave pure spiritual milk, so that by it you may grow up in your salvation."
1 Peter 2:2

Move on to solids

"In fact, though by this time you ought to be teachers, you need someone to teach you the elementary truths of God's word all over again. You need milk, not solid food! Anyone who lives on milk, being still an infant, is not acquainted with the teaching about righteousness. But solid food is for the mature, who by constant use have trained themselves to distinguish good from evil." *Hebrews 5:12-14*

Honey

"They [the ordinances of the Lord] are sweeter than honey, than honey from the comb."
Psalm 19:10

"How sweet are your words to my taste, sweeter than honey to my mouth." *Psalm 119:103*

Job treasured God's Word

"I have not departed from the commands of his lips; I have treasured the words of his mouth more than my daily bread."
Job 23:12

Jeremiah ate the words of God

"When your words came, I ate them; they were my joy and my heart's delight." *Jeremiah 15:16*

"From infancy"

It is never too early to read and teach the Bible to children. Paul once alluded to Timothy's early acquaintance with the Scriptures.

> "From infancy you have known the holy Scriptures, which are able to make you wise for salvation through faith in Jesus Christ." *2 Timothy 3:15*

From grandparent to parent to child

Parents and grandparents have the privilege and responsibility of teaching the Bible in their family circle.

Paul tells us that Timothy benefitted from such a godly upbringing:

Abraham Lincoln's testimony

"I believe that the Bible is the best gift that God has ever given to man. All the good from the Savior of the world is communicated to us through this book. I have been driven many times to my knees by the overwhelming conviction that I had nowhere else to go."
16th President of the United States.

> "I have been reminded of your sincere faith, which first lived in your grandmother Lois and your mother Eunice and, I am persuaded, now lives in you also." *2 Timothy 1:5*

Making the most of daily Bible reading

Give yourself a check up

1. Am I delighting more in reading the Bible now than a year ago?

> **Advice from a martyr:** "Straightway a flame was kindled in my soul, and a love of the prophets and of those men who are friends of Christ, possessed me." *Justin Martyr*

2. Do I recall at any time during the day what I read from the Bible in the morning?

> **Advice from a philanthropist:** "The vigor of our spiritual life will be in exact proportion to the place held by the Bible in our life and thoughts." *George Müller*

3. What one thing can I do to make more progress with my daily Bible readings?

> **Advice from an evangelist:** "I never saw a useful Christian who was not a student of the Bible. If a person neglects the Bible there is not much for the Holy Spirit to work with. We must have the word." *Dwight L. Moody*

Search the Scriptures

From the S-E-A-R-C-H T-H-E S-C-R-I-P-T-U-R-E-S acrostic on the facing page, take one letter a day, for the next nineteen days, and see how the verse for that letter can help you improve or deepen your own daily Bible reading.

- Read the verses around it.
- With the help of a reference Bible look up verses that teach the same truth.
- Ask God to show you how it relates to your own life.

S-E-A-R-C-H T-H-E S-C-R-I-P-T-U-R-E-S

S-tudiously	"Do your best to present yourself to God as one . . . who correctly handles the word of truth." *2 Timothy 2:15*
E-arnestly	[THE ETHIOPIAN EUNUCH WAS] ". . . reading Isaiah the prophet . . . The eunuch asked Philip, 'Tell me, please, who is the prophet talking about?'" *Acts 8:34*
A-rdently	"My soul is consumed with longing for your laws at all times." *Psalm 119:20*
R-egularly	"The Bereans . . . examined the Scriptures every day." *Acts 17:11*
C-arefully	"Listen, my sons, to a father's instruction; pay attention and gain understanding." *Proverbs 4:1*
H-umbly	"Do not merely listen to the word . . . Do what it says." *James 1:22*
T-hankfully	"At midnight I rise to give you thanks for your righteous laws." *Psalm 119:62*
H-appily	"The precepts of the LORD are right, giving joy to the heart." *Psalm 19:8*
E-agerly	"I run in the path of your commands, for you have set my heart free." *Psalm 119:32*
S-ystematically	"And beginning with Moses and all the Prophets, . . ." *Luke 24:27*
C-onscientiously	". . . a workman . . . who correctly hands the word of truth." *2 Timothy 2:15*
R-ichly	"Let the word of Christ dwell in you richly . . ." *Colossians 3:16*
I-ntently	"Applying your heart to understanding." *Proverbs 2:2*
P-rayerfully	"Open my eyes that I may see wonderful things in your law." *Psalm 119:18*
T-rustingly	"I believe everything that . . . is written in the Prophets." *Acts 24:14*
U-nashamedly	"I will not be put to shame when I consider all your commands." *Psalm 119:6*
R-etentively	"I have hidden your word in my heart." *Psalm 119:11*
E-xpectantly	"'My word . . . will accomplish what I desire.'" *Isaiah 55:11*
S-atisfyingly	"I have treasured the words of his mouth more than my daily bread." *Job 23:12*

Linking Bible reading and prayer

Listening and speaking

Some of us are better at pouring out our hearts to God in prayer than we are at listening to see what God has to say to us as we read the Bible.

Others of us are better at hearing God speaking to our consciences as we read his Word than we are at offering God genuine worship and praise or heartfelt petition, that we and those we love will live our lives in line with his word.

We are meant to be good at both.

> "I have sought your face with all my heart; be gracious to me according to your promise." *Psalm 119:58*

God's plan is for Bible reading and prayer to always be linked.

Phylacteries

Phylacteries were small leather boxes which pious Jews strapped to their foreheads and their left hands as they prayed. Inside these boxes were small passages of Scripture: *Exodus 13:1-10; 13:11-16; Deuteronomy 6:4-9; 11:13-21.*

Jesus spoke against the misuse of phylacteries by the teachers of the law and the Pharisees. God had originally given the idea of the phylacteries to his people to help them link his word to their lives.

> " 'Everything they do is done for men to see: they make their phylacteries wide.' " *Matthew 23:5*

"Tie them as symbols . . ."

"Hear, O Israel: The LORD our God, the LORD is one. Love the LORD your God with all your heart and with all your soul and with all your strength. These commandments that I give you today are to be upon your hearts. Impress them on your children. Talk about them when you sit at home and when you walk along the road, when you lie down and when you get up. Tie them as symbols on your hands and bind them on your foreheads. Write them on the doorframes of your houses and on your gates." *Deuteronomy 6:4-9*

Praying words of Scripture

When Jesus was on the cross, one of his prayers was a direct quotation from Psalm 22:1.

> "About the ninth hour Jesus cried out in a loud voice, 'Eloi, Eloi, lama sabachthani?' – which means, 'My God, my God, why have you forsaken me?'" *Matthew 27:46*

Model prayers in the Bible

There are many prayers in the Bible which are ideal for you to use in your times of prayer.

Theme of prayer	Bible reference
For believers	*Ephesians 1:16-23*
Prayer of confession	*Psalm 51*
Prayer of praise	*Luke 1:46-55*
Prayer of dedication	*2 Chronicles 6:14-42*
Prayer for blessing	*Psalm 90*
For times of despair	*Psalm 73*

"The soul will grow lean"

"I suspect I have been allotting habitually too little time to religious exercises, as private devotion and religious meditation, Scripture-reading, etc.

"Hence I am lean and cold and hard. I had better allot two hours or an hour and a half daily. I have been keeping too late hours, and hence have had but a hurried half-hour in the morning to myself. Surely the experience of all good men confirms the proposition that without a measure of private devotions the soul will grow lean."
William Wilberforce

Sorting out problems encountered in the Bible

Loss of confidence

It is important that you do not lose confidence in the fact that the Bible is God's Word, even though you may encounter what appears to be a problem in it.

Even if you have no problems with the Bible at present, you may find these two pages helpful as a means of helping others.

Back to basics

No matter what complex questions may arise from the Bible, remember that the Bible claims to be a divinely inspired book.

> "All Scripture is God-breathed and is useful for teaching, rebuking, correcting and training in righteousness, so that the man of God may be thoroughly equipped for every good work." *2 Timothy 3:16-17*

The Bible does not all of a sudden become uninspired because our weak, feeble brains can't cope with a simple difficulty or fathom a profound truth.

Admit to difficulties

Sometimes a Bible teacher may give the impression that the Bible's integrity is being attacked if one admits to having any problems about understanding it. Jesus's first disciples did not understand his resurrection.

> "He said to them, 'How foolish you are, and how slow of heart to believe all that the prophets have spoken! Did not the Christ have to suffer these things and then enter his glory?' And beginning with Moses and all the Prophets, he explained to them what was said in all the Scriptures concerning himself." *Luke 24:25-26*

Some of our difficulties about the Bible arise more from our own lack of spiritual insight and knowledge of Scripture than any inherent contradiction with the Bible itself.

The Bible is sometimes hard to understand

Even Peter said that some of the apostle Paul's letters were not easy to understand.

Peter once wrote about Paul's letters in this way:

> "His letters contain some things that are hard to understand." *2 Peter 3:16*

There is no shame attached to not understanding everything we read in the Bible.

The Bible is a book about salvation

Many of the difficulties we have with the Bible are of our own making and are not the fault of the Bible.

Learned professors may write dissertations about who wrote the letter to the Hebrews. Was Paul the author? Or was it someone other than Paul? Was it Apollos? But this so-called questioning does not affect our souls. As Peter wrote,

> "Bear in mind that our Lord's patience means salvation, just as our dear brother Paul also wrote you with the wisdom that God gave him." *2 Peter 3:15*

People love to attack the Bible

Some things never change! In Peter's day people lashed out against Scripture, just as they do today. The Bible and its contents are being continually challenged.

> "He [Paul] writes the same way in all his letters, speaking in them of these matters. His letters contain some things that are hard to understand, which ignorant and unstable people distort, as they do the other Scriptures, to their own destruction." *2 Peter 3:16*

Be on guard

Attacks on the Bible do not harm the Bible, but we should be aware of them. Peter went on to write:

> "Therefore, dear friends, since you already know this, be on your guard so that you may not be carried away by the error of lawless men and fall from your secure position." *2 Peter 3:17*

Help from God

Jesus has promised the help of his Holy Spirit. Read *John 16:12-15.*

Using hymn books

Jesus sang hymns

"When they had sung a hymn, they went out to the Mount of Olives."
Matthew 26:30

Making use of a book of hymns

Most hymn books are divided into helpful sections.
Go to the section under Worship or Praise and pick a hymn you
can pray as you start your time of prayer.

Special hymns for special occasions

It's useful to browse the table of contents in a hymn book.
There you will often find headings such as: Morning, Evening,
Easter, the Sick. Find the one that fits the theme you want to
pray about.

Favorite hymns

Many of our favorite hymns express the truths of the Bible in a
most helpful way. Because we usually only sing hymns in
church, we often fail to ponder their words. Use Mrs C. F.
Alexander's hymn in your next time of prayer:

There is a green hill far away

There is a green hill far away,
    Outside a city wall,
Where the dear Lord was crucified
    Who died to save us all.

We may not know, we cannot tell,
    What pains he had to bear,
But we believe it was for us
    He hung and suffered there.

He died that we might be forgiven,
    He died to make us good;
That we might go at last to heaven,
    Saved by his precious blood.

O, dearly, dearly has he loved,
    And we must love him too,
And trust in his redeeming blood
    And try his works to do.

Sing the hymn throughout the day

Pick a hymn you love. Use it in your time of prayer and sing it to yourself throughout the day.

"Shall I be silent?"

The shepherds sing, and shall I be silent?
My God, no hymn for thee?
My soul's a shepherd too; a flock it feeds
Of thoughts and words and deeds:
The pasture of thy word; the streams of thy grace.
Enriching all the place.
Shepherds and flock shall sing, and all my powers
Out-sing the daylight hours.
George Herbert

Using books of prayers

C. S. Lewis

"A few formal, ready-made, prayers serve me as a corrective of – well, let's call it 'cheek' [foolhardy disregard for spiritual things]."
C. S. Lewis, Letters to Malcolm Chiefly on Prayer

C. S. Lewis is saying here that he found at times prewritten prayers helped him to have reverence for God as he set about praying.

A book of prayers

It is a good idea to use a use a book of written prayers during your own time of prayer.

They are often scriptural. They often reflect the spiritual life of godly people who have spent many years in developing and improving their fellowship with God.

Ancient prayers

Many of the oldest prayers are among the best prayers.

> Almighty God and gracious Father,
> give us wisdom to perceive you,
> diligence to seek you,
> patience to wait for you,
> eyes to behold you,
> a heart to meditate on you,
> and a life to proclaim you,
> through the power of the Spirit of Jesus Christ our Lord.
> *Benedict (480-547)*
>
> Eternal Light, shine into our hearts,
> Eternal Goodness, deliver us from evil,
> Eternal Power, be our support,
> Eternal Wisdom, scatter the darkness of our ignorance,
> Eternal Pity, have mercy upon us;
> that with all our heart and mind and soul and strength
> we may seek your face and be brought by your infinite mercy
> to your holy presence; through Jesus Christ our Lord.
> *Alcuin of York (735-804)*

Devotional praying

Ah, Lord God, you holy lover of my soul, when you come into my soul, all that is within me rejoices. You are my glory and the exultation of my heart; you are my hope, and refuge in the day of my trouble. Set me free from all evil passions, and heal my heart of all excessive desires; that being inwardly cured and thoroughly cleansed, I may be made fit to love, courageous to suffer, steady to persevere.

Nothing is sweeter than love, nothing more courageous, nothing fuller nor better in heaven and earth; because love is born of God, and cannot rest but in God, above all created things. Let me love you more than myself, and not love myself except for you; and in you all that truly love you, as the law of love commands, shining out from yourself.

Thomas à Kempis

Extempore prayer

Tertullian, who lived at the end of the second century, A.D. 150-212, wrote,

> "We pray without a prompter because [we pray] from the heart."

But he also used written prayers. Written prayers and extemporaneous prayers are useless, unless they are both from the heart.

Praying all day long

How is this possible?

The apostle Paul told the Christians at Thessalonica to, "pray continually." *1 Thessalonians 5:17*

But how are we meant to do this? Clearly we are not meant to enter into a twenty-four hour marathon of non-stop prayer. Paul means we are to have an attitude of prayer and dependence on God, so that we can naturally pray to God at any time during the day.

Abraham's servant

Ishmael thanked God after his prayer about finding a bride for Isaac was answered.

> "Then the man bowed down and worshiped the LORD, saying, 'Praise be to the LORD, the God of my master Abraham, who has not abandoned his kindness and faithfulness to my master.'"
> *Genesis 24:26-27*

Questions to ponder:
• Do you naturally turn to God in gratitude when any of your prayers are answered?
• Would you know if God quit answering prayers?

Hannah's psalm of praise

Hannah expressed her thankfulness to God for the birth of Samuel, but it was not a brief, "Thank you, Lord:"

> "My heart rejoices in the LORD;
>   in the LORD my horn is lifted high.
> My mouth boasts over my enemies,
>   for I delight in your deliverance.
> There is no one holy like the LORD;
>   there is no one beside you;
>   there is no Rock like our God. . . .
> She who was barren has borne seven children,
>   but she who has many sons pines away. . . .
> For the foundations of the earth are the LORD's;
>   upon them he has set the world.
> He will guard the feet of his saints,
>   but the wicked will be silenced in darkness.
> It is not by strength that one prevails;
>   those who oppose the LORD will be shattered."
> *1 Samuel 2:1-2, 5, 8-10*

Learning from the prayers in the Bible

Re-read Hannah's prayer, looking for two things:

1. Expressions of Hannah's personal devotion to the Lord.
2. The different things we are told about God from this prayer.

Sentence prayers

Nehemiah is one of the first examples in the Bible of someone using sentence prayers. These are usually short prayers which are prayed on the spur of the moment, at any time during the day. By developing this habit you will be "praying continually."

1. When asked a crucial question, Nehemiah prayed before answering.
   "The king said to me, 'What is it you want?' Then I prayed to the God of heaven, and I answered the king . . ."
   Nehemiah 2:4-5

2. Nehemiah prayed as he worked.
   "But we prayed to our God and posted a guard day and night to meet this threat." *Nehemiah 4:9*

3. When he was in danger of giving in, he prayed,
   "They were all trying to frighten us, thinking, 'Their hands will get too weak for the work and it will not be completed.' But I prayed, 'Now strengthen my hands.'"
   Nehemiah 6:9

Being silent before God

The lack of silence

Silence and quietness is missing in many services of worship. You can be quiet and prayerful before a church service, seeking God's forgiveness and remembering God's presence rather than adding to the noise by talking with everyone around you.

A wise saying from the book of Ecclesiastes reminds us,

> "There is . . . a time to be silent and a time to speak."
> *Ecclesiastes 3:1, 7*

Being still

To be still means to silence the stream of words, thoughts, and images that go on in your own mind.

> "And when you pray, do not keep on babbling like pagans, for they think they will be heard because of their many words." *Matthew 6:7*

The prophets commend silence

1. Zechariah	"'Be still before the LORD, all mankind, because he has roused himself from his holy dwelling.'" *Zechariah 2:13*
2. Isaiah	"'Be silent before me, you islands.'" *Isaiah 41:1*
3. Habakkuk	"'But the LORD is in his holy temple; let all the earth be silent before him.'" *Habakkuk 2:20*
4. Zephaniah	"'Be silent before the Sovereign LORD, for the day of the Lord is near.'" *Zephaniah 1:7*

Be still in order to hear God

"'Be still, and know that I am God.'" *Psalm 46:10*

Silence and confession of sin

"When you are on your beds, search your hearts and be silent." *Psalm 4:4*

The still small voice

It is possible to be so active and to live our lives in such a rush that we miss God's voice speaking to us.

> "The Lord said, 'Go out and stand on the mountain in the presence of the Lord, for the Lord is about to pass by.'" *1 Kings 19:11*

Elijah had to listen and listen. For God was not in the wind, or the earthquake, or the fire. God was to be heard in the gentle whisper.

A gentle whisper

"And after the fire came a gentle whisper. When Elijah heard it, he pulled his cloak over his face and went out and stood at the mouth of the cave." *1 Kings 19:12-13*

The need for prayer for God's help

"To you I call, O Lord my Rock; do not turn a deaf ear to me. For if you remain silent, I shall be like those who have gone down to the pit." *Psalm 28:1*

Silence sometimes speaks louder than words. And it is only in a silence that we hear God's gentle whisper.

The need for forgiveness

God is sometimes silent because we have refused to listen to what he has already said.

> "'But since you rejected me when I called and no one gave heed when I stretched out my hand, since you ignored all my advice and would not accept my rebuke, I in turn will laugh at your disaster; . . . Then they will call to me but I will not answer; they will look for me but will not find me. Since they hated knowledge and did not choose to fear the LORD, since they would not accept my advice and spurned my rebuke, they will eat the fruit of their ways and be filled with the fruit of their schemes.'"
> *Proverbs 1:24-26; 28-31*

Practicing the presence of God

God's presence amid everyday activities

"The time of business does not with me differ from the time of prayer; and in the noise and clatter of my kitchen, while several people are at the same time calling for different things, I possess God in as great tranquillity as if I were upon my knees." *Brother Lawrence*

Worship in heaven

In worship we practice the presence of God. Go through the following references from the book of Revelation and note how the great congregation of heaven is taken up with praising God.

- *Revelation 4:8, 11*
- *Revelation 5:9-14*
- *Revelation 7:9-17*
- *Revelation 11:16-18*
- *Revelation 12:10-12*
- *Revelation 15:3-4*
- *Revelation 16:5-7*
- *Revelation 19:1-8*

Turn stumblingblocks into steppingstones

Whenever a difficulty sneaks up, turn that difficulty into a prayer and a way of knowing more of God's power.

". . . in everything, by prayer and petition, with thanksgiving, present your requests to God." *Philippians 4:6*

Rainbows

Many things in the universe can often remind us
of God's presence.

	The rainbow in Genesis	The rainbow in Ezekiel	The rainbow in Revelation
Where?	Genesis 9:9-17	Ezekiel 1:26-28	Revelation 4:1-3
Purpose?	God's covenant	To show God's glory	To reveal God's majesty
Position?	In the clouds	Above the expanse	Around God's throne
Shape?	Semi-circle	Arch	Full circle

Every rainbow we see should remind us of God's presence.
On earth rainbows are seen as half circles, but from outside the
earth they are seen as circles, highlighting perfection and
completeness.

Responding to God's presence

"Having found in many books
different methods of going to
God, and diverse practices of the
spiritual life, I thought this would
serve rather to puzzle me than
facilitate what I sought after,
which was nothing but how to
become wholly God's.

"I began to live as though there
was none but he and I in the
world. I worshiped him as often as
I could, keeping my mind in his
holy presence." *Brother Lawrence*

What to do when you don't want to pray

Be honest

Tell God how you feel. One of the remarkable characteristics of the psalmist is that he is open about his sadness, anxiety, and even his complaints against God.

The depressed psalmist

The psalmist states, "My soul is downcast within me." He also reveals his spiritual state when he asks himself, "Why are you downcast, O my soul: Why so disturbed within me?"

But he then tells himself what to do:

"Put your hope in God, for I will yet praise him, my Savior and my God." *Psalm 42:5*

Praise God

When we do not feel like praying it may seem strange to say that what we must do is to praise God. But this is what the psalmist did in the above example.

God does not love us less when we feel distant from him. God's love is not diminished when we just don't want to make the effort to pray.

Praise God for who he is

So next time you don't want to pray, remember who God is and praise him for who he is and for what he is able to do.

1. God is able to help you in temptation.
   "Because he [Jesus] himself suffered when he was tempted, he is able to help those who are being tempted." *Hebrews 2:18*
2. God is able to raise the downtrodden.

"The LORD upholds all those who fall and lifts up all who are bowed down." *Psalm 145:14*

3. God is able guard our souls.
   "That is why I am suffering as I am. Yet I am not ashamed, because I know whom I have believed, and am convinced that he is able to guard what I have entrusted to him for that day." *2 Timothy 1:12*

Give thanks

Another antidote to feeling down in the dumps spiritually is to give thanks to God.

"Give thanks in all circumstances, for this is God's will for you in Christ Jesus." *1 Thessalonians 5:18*

This verse has been paraphrased, "Alleluia anyway."

Gratitude

"Let gratitude for the past inspire us with trust for the future." *F. Fénelon*

"See that you do not forget what you were before, lest you take for granted the grace and mercy your received from God and forget to express your gratitude each day." *Martin Luther*

Recall what Jesus is doing for you

1. Jesus is praying for you.
   "Therefore he is able to save completely those who come to God through him, because he always lives to intercede for them." *Hebrews 7:25*
2. Jesus speaks to the Father on your behalf.
   "My dear children, I write this to you so that you will not sin. But if anybody does sin, we have one who speaks to the Father in our defense – Jesus Christ, the Righteous One." *1 John 2:1*

Pass it on

Revival in Rwanda

During the height of one of the
revivals in Rwanda, Christians
were noted for asking each
other the following question:
What have you learned about
Jesus or God today?

Is that a question you could
ask and/or answer each day?

Live it out

A pond goes stagnant if there
is no outlet. Ask yourself:

- Have I unwittingly become
  slack in obeying God?
- Have I allowed some sin or
  failure to creep into my life?
- Have I forgotten that I follow
  a Master who "went around
  doing good"? *Acts 10:38*

Speak out

Your devotional life will be
enhanced when you begin
witnessing about God in your
life.

This is not to say that we
witness in order to have a
closer walk with God, but that
one definite result from
sharing your faith will be that
your own spiritual life will be
strengthened.

> ". . . proclaiming aloud your
> praise
> and telling of all your wonderful
> deeds."
> *Psalm 26:7*

Sharing your praises of God

- Praise was a characteristic
  of God's people in the Old
  Testament.

> "Then we your people,
>   the sheep of your pasture,
>   will praise you forever;
> from generation to generation
>   we will recount your praise."
> *Psalm 79:13*

- Praise was also a
  characteristic of the early
  Christians.

> ". . . as you sing psalms,
> hymns and spiritual songs
> with gratitude in your hearts
> to God." *Colossians 3:16*

What to say

Characteristic	Example
1. The truth	". . . speaking the truth in love . . ." *Ephesians 4:15*
2. What you know of Jesus in your life	"You will be my witnesses in Jerusalem, and in all Judea and Samaria, and to the ends of the earth." *Acts 1:8*
3. The word of Jesus	"Let the word of Christ dwell in you richly as you teach and admonish one another with all wisdom . . ." *Colossians 3:16*
4. Speak about God's glory	"And in his temple all cry, 'Glory!'" *Psalm 29:9*
5. What is right	"He who walks righteously and speaks what is right . . ." *Isaiah 33:15*

How to say it

Characteristic	Example
1. Wholesomely	"Let your conversation be always . . . seasoned with salt." *Colossians 4:6*
2. Boldly	"When they saw the courage of Peter and John." *Acts 4:13*
3. With love	". . . speaking the truth in love . . ." *Ephesians 4:15*
4. With grace	"Let your conversation be always full of grace." *Colossians 4:7*

Compelled to speak

The first Christians had no problems about witnessing. They were propelled along by the Holy Spirit and found that speaking about God and Jesus was quite normal and natural. When the Sanhedrin counsel told Peter and John, "not to speak or teach at all in the name of Jesus," Peter and John responded fearlessly, ". . . we cannot but help speaking about what we have heard and seen." *Acts 4:18-20*

Listening to the Bible on cassette

How to grow
It is possible to listen to God's Word in a variety of ways: through reading the Bible, through hearing sermons, and through reading books explaining the Bible.

You should also literally listen to God's Word.

> "Come, my children, listen to me;
> I will teach you the fear of the LORD."
> *Psalm 34:11*

Bible on cassette or CD is readily available
Have you ever thought about purchasing the Bible on cassette from a local Christian Bookstore? (Hendrickson Publishers produce both Bible on cassette and Bible on CD by Alexander Scourby and Stephen Johnston.)

Or you may find it refreshing to listen to part of God's Word spoken in a Bible version you are not familiar with. Different versions are available today.

It will surprise you how different and how meditative it can be to listen to someone reading the Bible on cassette or CD.

Do it yourself
If you have a cassette recorder you can record part of the Bible and listen to it over and over again as you do routine jobs, drive in your car or exercise.

Try recording Paul's letter to the Philippians. It only takes a short time to record.
"Let me meditate on the teachings of your precepts." *Psalm 119:27*

Speak along with the cassette
When you are listening to a familiar passage of Scripture on your cassette, speak along with the voice on the cassette and let the thoughts seep into your soul.
You can aim to become like the psalmist:

> "I delight in your commands because I love them. I lift up my hands to your commands, which I love, and I meditate on your decrees." *Psalm 119:47-48*

Which parts of Scripture should I listen to?
- Start with the four gospels and the psalms.
- Then try Paul's letters.
- Then move on to the rest of the New Testament.
- Then listen to the prophets of the Old Testament.
- Finally, listen to the rest of the Old Testament.

Read good sermons

Satan snatches God's Word from our hearts

In the parable of the sower, Jesus taught a very important truth about God's Word being snatched out of our hearts by Satan. Satan does not want us to be absorbed in the Scriptures and scriptural truths.

> "'Listen! A farmer went out to sow his seed. As he was scattering the seed, some fell along the path, and the birds came and ate it up. . . . Some people are like seed along the path, where the word is sown. As soon as they hear it, Satan comes and takes away the word that was sown in them.'" *Mark 4:3-4, 15*

Heard any good sermons lately?

You may be blessed by hearing one or two helpful sermons every Sunday. Or, you may be starving to hear a good message from God's Word.

Either way, you can supplement what you hear by reading pulpit discourses from books of sermons.

Martin Luther: On Faith And Coming To Christ

1. This Gospel text teaches exclusively of the Christian faith, and awakens that faith in us; just as John, throughout his whole Gospel, simply instructs us how to trust in Christ the Lord. This faith alone, when based upon the sure promises of God, must save us; as our text clearly explains. And in the light of it all, they must become fools who have taught us other ways to become godly. All that human ingenuity can devise, be it as holy and as luminous as it may, must tumble to the ground if man be saved in God's way – in a way different from that which man himself plans. Man may forever do as he will, he can never enter heaven unless God takes the first step with his Word, which offers him divine grace and enlightens his heart so as to get upon the right way.

2. This right way, however, is the Lord Jesus Christ. Whoever desires to seek another way, as the great multitudes venture to do by means of their own works, has already missed the right way; for Paul says to the Galatians: "If righteousness is through the law" that is, through the works of the Law, "then Christ died for nothing" (*Galatians 2:21*). Therefore I say man must fall upon this Gospel and be broken

Go for the giants

Endless books of sermons are published. Some are excellent and provide a wealth of uplifting material, while other sermon books provide little depth.

We encourage you to go for the giant preachers of the past. Beg, borrow, or steal a book of sermons by Martin Luther, C. H. Spurgeon, Andrew Murray, F. B. Meyer, G. Cambell Morgan, or Dr. Martyn Lloyd-Jones.

to pieces and in deep consciousness lie prostrate, like a man that is powerless, unable to move hand or foot. He must only lie motionless and cry: Almighty God, merciful Father, now help me! I cannot help myself. Christ, my Lord, do help now, for with only my own effort all is lost! Thus, in the light of this cornerstone, which is Christ, everyone becomes as nothing; as Christ says of himself in Luke 20:17-18, when he asks the Pharisees and scribes: "What then is this that is written. The stone which the builders rejected, the same was made the head of the corner? Every one that falleth on that stone shall be "broken to pieces; but on whomsoever it shall fall, it will scatter him as dust" (*Psalm 118:22*). Therefore, we must either fall upon this stone, Christ, in all our inability and helplessness, rejecting our own merits, and be broken to pieces, or he will forever crush us by his severe sentence and judgment. It is better that we fall upon him than that he should fall upon us. For this reason the Lord says in this Gospel, "No man can come to me, except the Father that sent me draw him: and I will raise him up in the last day." (*John 6:44*)

Listen to inspiring Christian singing

"I can't sing"

It doesn't matter whether you can carry a tune when you sing or not . . . when it comes to listening to Christian singing. What matters is where your heart is.

"Sing and make music in you heart to the Lord." *Ephesians 5:19*

Cassettes and CDs

Borrow, buy, or record a Christian hymn or song you find especially spiritually uplifting. Sing along with it as you play it. Pray its words as you listen to it and think about what the words mean.

America's favorite hymn

Amazing grace, how sweet the sound
That saved a wretch like me,
I once was lost, but now am found,
Was blind, but now I see.

'Twas grace that taught my heart to fear,
And grace my fears relieved.
How precious did that grace appear
The hour I first believed.

Through many dangers, toils and snares,
I have already come.
'Tis grace hath brought me safe thus far,
And grace will lead me home.

The story behind the hymn
Find out through books or the Internet how some of your favorite hymns came to be written.

John Newton
The story of John Newton, author of *Amazing Grace*, is an amazing story indeed. The hymn is the story of his Christian conversion and his Christian life.

Newton was in a slaveship in the middle of a storm which threatened to sink his ship. He found Thomas à Kempis's *Imitation of Christ* on board, read it, and later committed his life to Christ.

Extravagant language
People have, at times, criticized Newton for using a word like "wretch" in this hymn. But this is exactly how Newton felt, and he never wanted to forget it. So in his hymn he was determined to show that before we are Christians we are indeed wretches (miserable, unhappy people)!

Grace
Newton spent the last forty-three years of his life preaching the gospel. At eighty-two, Newton said, "My memory is nearly gone, but I remember two things, that I am a great sinner, and that Christ is a great Savior."

No wonder his famous hymn focused on God's amazing grace.

Making the secular sacred

An unreal division

We are used to dividing things up in our thinking into the secular (worldly) and the sacred (spiritual).

But as God is the Creator and the Sustainer of the universe, everything belongs to him. So in that sense everything can be sacred for Christians.

Stars

"Praise him, sun and moon,
praise him, all you shining stars."
Psalm 148:3

When you see the heavens full of glimmering stars, or a wonderful sunset, don't just exclaim: "How beautiful!" Praise God in your hearts and thank your Creator for his wonderful world.

Rain

Next time you feel like grumbling because it is raining, praise God, not only because we need rain and many parts of the world are devastated by drought, but also because rain is pictured as a sign of God's blessing.

"You gave abundant showers,
O God;
your refreshed your weary
    inheritance."
Psalm 68:9

"Blessed are those whose
strength is in you,
who have set their hearts on
    pilgrimage.
As they pass through the Valley
    of Baca,
they make it a place of springs;
the autumn rains also cover it
    with pools.
They go from strength to
    strength,
till each appears before God in
    Zion."
Psalm 84:5-7

Reaping

When you see corn being harvested you can praise God, your Provider. Even if you never see a field of corn, you can thank God for his provision each time you go into a supermarket.

> "You care for the land and water it;
> you enrich it abundantly.
> The streams of God are filled with water
> to provide the people with grain, for so you have ordained it."
> *Psalm 65:9*

Mountains

Everyday sights reminded the psalmist of who God is. Jesus used objects found in everyone's home like yeast, jewelry, lamps and salt, to illustrate eternal truths.

You can do the same as you allow objects and nature to remind you about God during your day.

- **Mountains and God's righteousness**
  "Your righteousness is like the mighty mountains,
  your justice like the great deep."
  Psalm 36:6

- **Pottery and God's power over our lives**
  " 'Like clay in the hand of the potter, so are you in my hand, O house of Israel.' "
  Jeremiah 18:6

Making the most of Christian festivals

Jesus went to the Temple for a festival

"Every year his parents went to Jerusalem for the Feast of the Passover. When Jesus was twelve years old, they went up to the Feast, according to the custom." *Luke 2:41-42*

Reliving God's saving acts

The people of Israel were taught by God to remember how they were rescued from slavery in Egypt by him. They were to do this in such a vivid way that they could experience the event again each year, as if it was happening to them.

"Celebrate the Passover"

"Observe the month of Abib and celebrate the Passover of the LORD your God, because in the month of Abib he brought you out of Egypt by night. Sacrifice as the Passover to the LORD your God an animal from your flock or herd at the place the LORD will choose as a dwelling for his Name. Do not eat it with bread made with yeast, but for seven days eat unleavened bread, the bread of affliction, because you left Egypt in haste – so that all the days of your life you may remember the time of your departure from Egypt. Let no yeast be found in your possession in all your land for seven days."
Deuteronomy 16:1-4

The Lord's Supper

In the New Testament we are taught that in the Lord's Supper we remember Christ delivered us from the power of death and that he is returning again.

"For whenever you eat this bread and drink this cup, you proclaim the Lord's death until he comes." *1 Corinthians 11:26*

Christmas and Easter

Of course, every day is a day to celebrate the coming of Jesus; and every Sunday is a resurrection day. But we can also make sure that we make the most of Advent, Christmas, Easter, Ascension Day, and Pentecost.

You and your local fellowship

Are you a strong supporter of your local Christian fellowship?
It is at the local church where the Christian festivals are
celebrated, including the celebration of Sunday as a holy day
and resurrection day. And that is one way of witnessing to the
world around about your dependence on a great and powerful
and loving God.

• Do you think that meeting with other Christians is an optional
  extra?

> "I rejoiced with those who said to me,
>   'Let us go to the house of the LORD.'" *Psalm 122:1*

A special promise

Jesus is with us always, but he
especially gives a promise that he
will be present where Christians
meet togther.

> "'For where two or three come
> together in my name, there am I with
> them.'" *Matthew 18:20*

Making the most of a restless night

Praise God

No matter how ill, upset, or worried you are, there is one positive thing you can do during a restless night. You can praise God.

> "Let the saints . . . sing for joy on their beds."
> *Psalm 149:5*

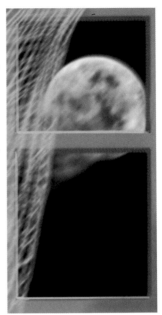

"Songs of the night"

Job had many restless nights as he struggled to come to terms with what he thought of as undeserved suffering. One of his counselors, Elihu, refers to "songs in the night" which he saw as a gift from God.

> "Men cry out under a load of
>   oppression;
>   they plead for relief from the
>   arm of the powerful.
> But no one says, 'Where is God my Maker,
>   who gives songs in the night.'"
> *Job 35:9-10*

The causes of a restless night

You may have little control over external circumstances like noise, illness, or heat which cause sleepless nights. But many restless nights are caused by internal matters which keep our minds so preoccupied that sleep evades us. You may need to talk with a Christian friend about why you can't sleep.

Worry

Everyone worries.

Jesus said some harsh words about worry, asserting that we are like pagans when we worry. But he also told us that because of his heavenly Father's care for us we need not worry.

We have to keep on recalling these words of Jesus by applying them to ourselves time and time again.

"Do not worry"

" 'Therefore I tell you, do not worry about your life, what you will eat or drink; or about your body, what you will wear. Is not life more important than food, and the body more important than clothes? Look at the birds of the air; they do not sow or reap or store away in barns, and yet your heavenly Father feeds them. Are you not much more valuable than they? Who of you by worrying can add a single hour to his life?' " *Matthew 6:25-27*

Do not worry about your future

"And why do you worry about clothes? See how the lilies of the field grow. They do not labor or spin. Yet I tell you that not even Solomon in all his splendor was dressed like one of these. If that is how God clothes the grass of the field, which is here today and tomorrow is thrown into the fire, will he not much more clothe you, O you of little faith?

So do not worry, saying,
'What shall we eat?' or
'What shall we drink?' or
'What shall we wear?'
For the pagans run after all these things, and your heavenly Father knows that you need them. But seek first his kingdom and his righteousness, and all these things will be given to you as well.

Therefore do not worry about tomorrow, for tomorrow will worry about itself. Each day has enough trouble of its own." *Matthew 6:28-34*

Do not give in to worry

"Do not fret – it leads only to evil." *Psalm 37:8*

"Tomorrow makes today's whole head sick, its whole heart faint. When we should be still, sleeping or dreaming, we are fretting about an hour that lies a half sun's journey away! Not so doest thou, Lord." *George Macdonald*

Reading Christian books

How to read
"If you would benefit, read with humility, simplicity and faith and never seek the fame of being learned." *Thomas à Kempis*

Books on doctrine
Institutes of the Christian Religion, by John Calvin, is still unsurpassed as a systematic summary of Bible teaching. It's lengthy two volumes may seem quite daunting, but there are shorter edited versions available.

Missionary books
Missionary books are extremely challenging and are often ideal books to lend to others.

Books by or about Hudson Taylor, who founded the China Inland Mission (now the Overseas Missionary Fellowship), John and Betty Stam, Jim Elliot, and the Auca Indians are all inspiring.

Missionary magazines
Do you take a missionary magazine? It is one way to prayerfully support today's missionaries.

Diaries
One of the most famous and moving diaries is the one written by David Brainerd concerning his pioneer missionary work among the American Indians.

Journals
Perhaps the two most famous Christian journals are those by John Wesley and George Whitefield. These journals give an accurate record of God's work of revival in England and America in the eighteenth-century.

Biographies and autobiographies
There are many biographies on great Christian leaders of the past, like Augustine of Hippo, Martin Luther, John Calvin, John Bunyan, and Jonathan Edwards.

Contemporary biographies and autobiographies on such people as Corrie ten Boom and Billy Graham illustrate how God continues to use people today.

A page a day

Some devotional and doctrinal books are best read slowly over a long period of time, rather than all in one sitting like a novel.

Try reading one or two pages a day from some classic Christian book. It does not matter if it takes you over a year to get to the end.

Preface to the letter to the Romans

Faith is a work of God in us, which changes us and brings us to birth anew from God (cf. John 1). It kills the old Adam, makes us completely different people in heart, mind, senses, and all our powers, and brings the Holy Spirit with it. What a living, creative, active powerful thing is faith! It is impossible that faith ever stop doing good. Faith doesn't ask whether good works are to be done, but, before it is asked, it has done them. It is always active. Whoever doesn't do such works is without faith; he gropes and searches about him for faith and good works but doesn't know what faith or good works are. Even so, he chatters on with a great many words about faith and good works.
Martin Luther

Reading Christian classics

Why read any other book than the Bible?

John Wesley, the Methodist preacher and Bible teacher, was known as "a man of one book," because he read and studied the Bible so much. But he also read a large number of other books, which greatly helped him in his ministry.

Charles Spurgeon, the Baptist preacher and Bible teacher, spent countless hours studying the Bible each week. But he also had a library consisting of many thousands of books which he read and used as he prepared his sermons.

"Meet with Christ"

"In your reading, let not your end be to seek and find out curiosities and subtleties, but to find and meet with Christ."
Thomas Taylor

"Christian devotional reading helps us find intimate union with God, its motivation being to love God with all our heart, mind and will." *Jonathan Edwards*

A short list of classic Christian books

- *Pilgrim's Progress*, John Bunyon
- *The Imitation of Christ*, traditionally attributed to Thomas à Kempis
- *A Treatise Concerning Religious Affections*, by Jonathan Edwards
- *The Book of Martyrs*, by John Foxe
- *The Confessions of Saint Augustine*
- *The Practice of the Presence of God*, by Brother Lawrence
- *Pensées*, by Blaise Pascal (see also pages 56–57)

"After the Bible itself, no book so profoundly influenced early Protestant sentiment as the Book of Martyrs. Even in our time it is still a living force." *James Miller Dodds*

"I am the wheat of Christ"

In this persecution suffered the blessed martyr, Ignatius, who is held in famous reverence among very many. This Ignatius was appointed to the bishopric of Antioch next after Peter in succession. Some do say, that he, being sent from Syria to Rome, because he professed Christ, was given to the wild beasts to be devoured.

It is also said of him, that when he passed through Asia, being under the most strict custody of his keepers, he strengthened and confirmed the churches through all the cities as he went, both with his exhortations and preaching of the Word of God.

Accordingly, having come to Smyrna, he wrote to the Church at Rome, exhorting them not to use means for his deliverance from martyrdom, lest they should deprive him of that which he most longed and hoped for.

"Now I begin to be a disciple. I care for nothing, of visible or invisible things, so that I may but win Christ. Let fire and the cross, let the companies of wild beasts, let breaking of bones and tearing of limbs, let the grinding of the whole body, and all the malice of the devil, come upon me; be it so, only may I win Christ Jesus!"

And even when he was sentenced to be thrown to the beasts, such was the burning desire that he had to suffer, that he spake, what time he heard the lions roaring, saying: "I am the wheat of Christ: I am going to be ground with the teeth of wild beasts, that I may be found pure bread."

Extract from The Book of Martyrs, John Foxe

The Holy Spirit and daily devotions (1)

Pause
• It's not always a good idea just to rush in and pray.
• Pause and remember to whom you are praying.
• Pause and remember who is helping you in your prayers – the Holy Spirit.

The ministry of the Holy Spirit
Jesus called the Holy Spirit the Counselor and promised that he would come after his ascension.
"'Unless I go away, the Counselor will not come to you; but if I go, I will send him to you.'" *John 16:7*

The tax collector and the Pharisee

Don't let you prayers degenerate into talking to yourself or telling God how good you are. In the parable of the Pharisee and the tax collector (*Luke 18:9-14*), Jesus gives a graphic picture of how not to pray.
"The Pharisee stood up and prayed about [*footnote:* to] himself: 'God, I thank you that I am not like other men – robbers, evildoers, adulterers – or even like this tax collector. I fast twice a week and give a tenth of all I get.'" *Luke 18:11-12*

Two ways of praying?
It is said that there are only two ways to pray. One is real prayer, the other is not prayer at all. So there is only one way to pray.
    You either pray in the Spirit, or you are not praying at all.
"Pray in the Spirit on all occasions." *Ephesians 6:18*

Do you feel empty and lifeless without the Spirit?
Remember the promise of Jesus.

> "'If you then, though you are evil, know how to give good gifts to your children, how much more will your Father in heaven give the Holy Spirit to those who ask him!'" *Luke 11:13*

Reflect on what the Holy Spirit does

The Spirit's ministry	Bible reference
1. He brings glory to Jesus	"'He will bring glory to me.'" *John 16:14*
2. He testifies about Jesus	"'He will testify about me.'" *John 15:26*
3. He brings spiritual life	"'The Spirit gives life.'" *John 6:63*
4. He lives in Christians	"'The Father . . . will give you another counselor to be with you for ever.'" *John 14:16*
5. He guides into truth	"'He will guide you into all truth.'" *John 16:13*
6. He teaches	"'The Holy Spirit . . . will teach you all things.'" *John 14:26*
7. He gives power for witnessing	"You will receive power when the Holy Spirit comes on you; and you will be my witnesses.'" *Acts 1:8*
8. He brings assurance	"We know that we live in him and he is us, because he has given us of his Spirit." *1 John 4:13*
9. He brings God's love	"God has poured out his love into our hearts by the Holy Spirit, whom he has given us." *Romans 5:5*
10. He builds up God's church	"Then the church throughout Judea, Galilee and Samaria enjoyed a time of peace. It was strengthened; and encouraged by the Holy Spirit, it grew in numbers, living in the fear of the Lord." *Acts 9:31*

The Holy Spirit
and daily devotions (2)

Help is at hand

The one person we need all the time in our daily devotions is the Holy Spirit.

As we draw near to God, so God draws near to us.

"Come near to God and he will come near to you." *James 4:8*

The Holy Spirit is said to help us in a specific way.

"Guard the good deposit [the gospel] that was entrusted to you – guard it with the help of the Holy Spirit who lives in us."
2 Timothy 1:14

The Holy Spirit lives in all Christians.
He is at hand to help us as we pray.

The result of being filled with the Spirit

Paul tells the Ephesians to be continually filled with the Spirit and not drunk with wine.

This results in spiritual songs and giving thanks to God.

". . . be filled with the Spirit.
Speak to one another with
psalms, hymns and spiritual songs.
Sing and make music in your heart to
the Lord,
always giving thanks to God the Father
for everything,
in the name of our Lord Jesus Christ."
Ephesians 5:18-20

Do you need help in your praying?

The apostle Paul assumes that the Christians at Rome needed divine assistance in their prayers.

We should always acknowledge our need here – or else we may lapse into thinking that we can pray on our own, without any help from God.

How the Holy Spirit helps you as you pray

Romans 8:26-27	Eight ways in which the Spirit helps
"In the same way, the Spirit helps us	**1.** He helps us. The Holy Spirit dwells in us and wants to help us as we pray
in our weakness.	**2.** We are naturally weak when it comes to prayer. We need to acknowledge this – or else we may not ask for divine assistance.
We do not know what we ought to pray for,	**3.** We will not always know how we should pray. We should ask the Holy Spirit to guide us.
but the Spirit himself intercedes for us	**4.** We are never alone as we pray. The Holy Spirit is with us and prays for us.
with groans that words cannot express.	**5.** "The best prayers are more often groans than words." *John Bunyan*
And he who searches our hearts knows the mind of the Spirit,	**6.** We are totally exposed to God's purifying light as we pray.
because the Spirit intercedes for the saints	**7.** The Holy Spirit knows all about us, and yet he prays to the Father on our behalf.
in accordance with God's will." *Romans 8:26-27*	**8.** The Holy Spirit's prayers are always in line with God's will – as ours should be.

57

Prayer is not a mechanism

Prayer is not a matter of ritual, or following a routine perfectly. Prayer is nothing if it does not have the breath of God's Spirit in it.

"The letter kills, but the Spirit gives life." *2 Corinthians 3:6*

As you awake

Your first conscious moments

As you wake, don't concentrate on how you feel. "Oh! I have a terrible headache!" or "What a wonderfully sunny day it is." Train yourself so that in your opening moments of consciousness you turn to Jesus and to his Word.

Read a verse from a psalm

If a verse does not come to your mind as you awake, turn to one from the psalms.

> "My heart is steadfast, O God,
>   my heart is steadfast;
>   I will make music.
> Away, my soul!
>   Awake, harp and lyre!
>   I will awaken the dawn."
> *Psalm 57:7-8*

Breathe a prayer of thanks

As you wake up, thank God for his goodness, and for the gift of another day.

> "How precious to me are your thoughts, O God!
> How vast is the sum of them!
> Were I to count them,
>   they would outnumber the grains of sand.
> When I awake,
>   I am still with you."
> *Psalm 139:17-18*

Worship first

Before you allow yourself to concentrate on the needs of your day, worship God. All these things only take seconds, but they may set the spiritual tone for your whole day. You are showing your dependence on God as you turn to him with your waking thoughts and as you pray to him.

> "But I will sing of your strength,
>   in the morning I will sing of your love;
> for you are my fortress,
>   my refuge in times of trouble."
> *Psalm 59:16*

Problems come second

• If you are besieged by a particular problem, ask God for his grace to face it today.

> "In the morning, O LORD, you hear my voice;
> in the morning I lay my requests before you
> and wait in expectation."
> *Psalm 5:3*

• If you are surrounded by many problems, now is the moment to commit them to God.

> "But I cry to you for help, O LORD;
> in the morning my prayer comes before you."
> *Psalm 88:13*

What to do when you are ill

Call for help

When you are ill, one important thing to remember is that you are part of a Christian fellowship and that God has provided other Christians to support, encourage, and help you.

Don't be bashful about phoning another Christian to ask for prayer.

The model in the letter of James

"Is any one of you in trouble? He should pray. Is anyone happy? Let him sing songs of praise. Is any one of you sick? He should call the elders of the church to pray over him and anoint him with oil in the name of the Lord. And the prayer offered in faith will make the sick person well; the Lord will raise him up. If he has sinned, he will be forgiven. Therefore confess your sins to each other and pray for each other so that you may be healed. The prayer of a righteous man is powerful and effective."
James 5:13-16

Remember Trophimus

Not all sickness will be instantly and miraculously cured. Even the apostle Paul did not manage to heal every sick person he ministered to.

"I left Trophimus sick in Miletus." *2 Timothy 4:20*

Learn from your illness

You may not be able to pray much or have enough strength to read your Bible. But that does not matter. See what spiritual lessons you can learn from your illness.

1. When your physical strength was taken away how did you react?
"My life is consumed by anguish
   and my years by groaning;
my strength fails because of my affliction,
   and my bones grow weak. . . .
But I trust in you, O LORD."
Psalm 31:10, 14

2. The example of Hezekiah
"I cried like a swift or thrush,
   I moaned like a mourning dove.
My eyes grew weak as I looked to the heavens.
   I am troubled; O Lord, come to my aid!"
. . . "The living, the living – they praise you,
   as I am doing today;
fathers tell their children about your faithfulness."
Isaiah 38:14,19

3. Can you say that your illness was in any sense a time of spiritual renewal?

"Therefore we do not lose heart. Though outwardly we are wasting away, yet inwardly we are being renewed day by day."
2 Corinthians 4:16

Paul and his thorn

Many people think that Paul's thorn was some kind of physical illness, perhaps linked to his eyes.

"To keep me from becoming conceited because of these surpassingly great revelations, there was given me a thorn in my flesh, a messenger of Satan, to torment me."

- **Paul asked God to remove this thorn**

"Three times I pleaded with the Lord to take it away from me."

- **Paul praised God for his weakness because through it he found God's power**

"But he said to me, 'My grace is sufficient for you, for my power is made perfect in weakness."
2 Corinthians 12:9

When you are well again

You may be more eager to visit and pray for your Christian friends when they are ill.

Don't give up

Prayer is a spiritual battle
"Satan trembles to see the weakest Christian on his or her knees."

Jesus knew we would want to give up
"Jesus told his disciples a parable to show them that they should always pray and not give up." *Luke 18:1*

Jesus then went on to tell the parable of the persistent widow. *(Luke 18:1-8)*

"Lord, teach us to pray"
We have seen that in response to the disciples' request, "Lord, teach us to pray, just as John taught his disciples to pray." Jesus told them how to pray, by giving them the prayer we now call The Lord's Prayer. *(Matthew 6:9-15; Luke 11:2-4)*

But what was the very next thing that Jesus taught about prayer?

Don't give up
Jesus went on to tell his disciples a parable about persistent prayer.

> "Then he said to them, 'Suppose one of you has a friend, and he goes to him at midnight and says, "Friend, lend me three loaves of bread, because a friend of mine on a journey has come to me, and I have nothing to set before him."
> 'Then the one inside answers, "Don't bother me. The door is already locked, and my children are with me in bed. I can't get up and give you anything." I tell you, though he will not get up and give him the bread because he is his friend, yet because of the man's boldness he will get up and give him as much as he needs.'"
> *Luke 11:7-8*

Don't be taken by surprise
From time to time, nearly everyone feels like skipping their daily devotions. If this happens to you, don't be overly surprised. If Jesus warned his first disciples that it would be tough to persevere in prayer, why should you think it would be any different for you?

"Ask, seek, knock"

After Jesus' parable about persistent prayer, he didn't leave the subject. He said, "'So I say to you: Ask and it will be given to you; seek and you will find; knock and the door will be opened to you. For everyone who asks receives; he who seeks finds; and to him who knocks, the door will be opened.'" *Luke 11:9-10*

Keep on keeping on.

Quotes from men of prayer

"When it is hardest to pray, we ought to pray the hardest."
D. L. Moody

"It is possible to move men, through God, by prayer alone."
Hudson Taylor

"A person's state before God may always be measured by his prayers. Whenever we begin to feel careless about our private prayers, we may depend on it, there is something very wrong in the condition of our souls. There are breakers ahead. We are in imminent danger of shipwreck."
J. C. Ryle

As you go to sleep

The night before
"The battle for the quiet time is won the night before." If you constantly stay up very late to watch TV programs don't be surprised if you find yourself missing your times of prayer in the morning.

Your spiritual state tomorrow morning will reflect your spiritual state tonight.

Don't dwell on your failures
Going to sleep can be a terrible time for people who are prone to depression.
- Do not allow yourself to think about any ways you have failed God.
- Do not dwell on anything negative.
- Meditate on God and the peace, comfort and hope he brings.

Your last waking thought
Try to make your last waking thought a prayer. Repeat in your heart and spirit a verse from the psalms.

"I will lie down and sleep in peace,
for you alone, O Lord,
make me dwell in safety."
Psalm 4:8

The God of hope
Turn Paul's prayer for the Christians at Rome into a prayer for yourself.

"May the God of hope fill you with all joy and peace as you trust in him, so that you may overflow with hope by the power of the Holy Spirit."
Romans 15:13

Scripture Memory
made easy

The only difficulty with remembering verses from the Bible is the lack of a little know-how.

Be clear about one thing: Scripture memory is not impossible.

Scripture memory made easy starts by assuming that you've never learned any Bible verses. But it ends up teaching you a lifetime's habit of storing God's Word in your heart.

Contents

Why bother learning Bible verses?

Memorizing Bible verses helps you:
- to understand God's Word
- to pray
- to meditate on God's Word
- to share Jesus with others
- to counter Satan's attacks

Remember it is God's Word

"For the word of God is living and active. Sharper than any double-edged sword, it penetrates even to dividing soul and spirit, joints and marrow; it judges the thoughts and attitudes of the heart."
Hebrews 4:12

Remember it is God's inspired Word

"But as for you, continue in what you have learned and have become convinced of, because you know those from whom you learned it, and how from infancy you have known the holy Scriptures, which are able to make you wise for salvation through faith in Christ Jesus. All Scripture is God-breathed and is useful for teaching, rebuking, correcting and training in righteousness, so that the man of God may be thoroughly equipped for every good work." *2 Timothy 3:14-17*

Motivation for memorizing scripture

You need to be motivated:
• to get you started
• so you won't give up

Don't worry if you think:

• **"My memory is terrible"** – this book will help you train your memory to remember Bible verses.
• **"I've tried it before"** – here is a simple way to help you, no matter how many times you may have tried to do this before.
• **"I don't know how to do this"** – this book gives you a step by step approach and assumes that you know nothing about memorizing Scripture.
• **"I've always wanted to memorize Scripture but I'm worried that I'll just give up"** – this book will keep on showing you how you can persevere in memorizing Scripture.

Motivation

What we enjoy doing most, we do best.

If you think of learning Bible verses merely as a laborious chore, you will find it much more difficult unless you realize that it will:
• help you become a stronger Christian
• help you to be more effective for Jesus.

Memorizing Scripture *is* hard work. It's no good starting to memorize Scripture thinking that it will be a breeze.

Perseverance is needed. But it is a joy and a privilege to draw closer to God in this way.

"The law of the LORD is perfect, reviving the soul.
The statutes of the LORD are trustworthy, making wise the simple.
The precepts of the LORD are right, giving joy to the heart.
The commands of the LORD are radiant, giving light to the eyes."
Psalm 19:7-8

Flawless . . . like pure gold

Memorizing Scripture is unlike memorizing anything else. Some of the techniques may be used when memorizing Shakespeare or reviewing for an exam.
But the *purpose* is different.
The *material* is unique.

> "And the WORDS of the Lord are flawless, like silver refined in a furnace of clay, purified seven times." *Psalm 12:6*

> "Because I love your commands more than gold, more than pure gold." *Psalm 119:127*

Build yourself up so you can help others

> "Let the word of Christ
> dwell in you richly
> as you teach
> and admonish one another with all wisdom,
> and as you sing psalms, hymns and spiritual songs
> with gratitude in your hearts to God."
> *Colossians 3:16*

What to do before you start

I. Pray

Ask God to help you as you prepare to undertake this task.

Ask God for his help as you memorize Scripture.

> "[God] answered their prayers, because they trusted in him."
> *1 Chronicles 5:20*

2. Be positive

You *can* memorize Scripture. Have a positive attitude as you start.

3. Which Bible should I use?

Use an accurate translation. Memorize all your verses in the same translation.

Use your current or favorite Bible as the basis for memorizing Scripture, but be certain that the translation is accurate. You probably should not use a paraphrase in scriptural memorization.

4. When should I memorize Scripture?

There are no rules here. Whenever is best for you is the best time. Some people make it part of the time while they are praying and reading their Bible. Some find first thing in the morning and last thing at night are good times for this.

5. Using memory cards

Obtain 100 white 3 x 5 index cards. Blank business cards sold by stationers are also ideal. You can carry them around with you in a little holder or credit card wallet.

Write one Bible verse on each card as you prepare to memorize it.

You may prefer to access the Bible verse on your computer and print it out in a small font on a stiff piece of paper which you can then cut up.

Then you are ready to carry around the verses with you at all times.

The Sadducees

The Sadducees in Jesus' day probably knew the Scriptures (our Old Testament) better than nearly all Christians today. But Jesus told them: "'You are in error because you do not know the Scriptures or the power of God'" *Matthew 22:29.* They knew the words of the Scripture, but in their hearts they did not know its meaning or its power.

As you memorize Scripture make sure that you don't think this will by itself make you a better Christian. Unless the verses sink into your soul, there will be little change in your life.

6. Remember your goal

Your goal in memorizing Scripture is to become more and more like Jesus. Keep this goal in mind for it is quite possible to memorize dozens of Bible verses and yet receive little or no spiritual benefit.

Do what the Word says

"Do not merely listen to the word, and so deceive yourselves. Do what it says. Anyone who listens to the word but does not do what it says is like a man who looks at his face in a mirror and, after looking at himself, goes away and immediately forgets what he looks like." *James 1:22-24*

Learning your first Bible verse

At last!
Now it is time to learn your first Bible verse. It's written out on this page as if it were on the card that you are going to write it on.

SIX KEYS	1/1/1
Loved by Jesus	

"As the Father has loved me, so have I loved you. Now remain in my love."
John 15:9

Learning the verse
Determine whether the verse divides into sections. This first verse has three sections.

- Start with the first phrase: As the Father has loved me. Learn that.
- Then memorize the second phrase: so have I loved you.
- Now see if you can say the first two phrases without looking at them.
- When you can, memorize the third phrase: Now remain in my love.
- Now try the whole verse. Keep on doing this until you're certain that you know the verse forward and backward!

Learning the Bible reference
If you are familiar with Bible references, you know that John 15:9 stands for where the verse comes in the Bible. John is for John's Gospel, 15 is for chapter 15, and 9 is for verse 9.

You should now memorize the reference. Then say the verse and its reference. Every time you learn a new Bible verse memorize its reference as well.

10

The Bible memory card

You will see five things on this card.

1. The top left hand corner has the words Six keys. This is the theme for the first six Bible verses you are going to learn. From the pull down chart at the end of the book you will see the next themes are: God's plan of salvation and Six "I am's" of Jesus.

2. The second line on the top left hand corner of the card says Loved by Jesus. This is the topic the verse deals with. This sub-heading helps you to see the point of the verse you are memorizing. These topic headings will also help you to remember all the different verses you have memorized.

3. The top right hand corner has 1/1/1. The first **1** stands for the year. The first year's worth of memory verses is year one. This **1** will only become **2** after you have learned 100 verses.

The second **1** refers to the week of the year you are in. As this is the first week you are learning a Bible verse it is week **1**. This means that you do not have to wait for January until you start. Week **1** is the week you start the course and that can be at any time in the year.

The third **1** indicates it is the first verse you have learned this week. These numbers help you to keep the cards in the order that you are learning the verses and put them back into that order should you drop them all!

4. The Bible verse itself is written out in the center of the card.

5. The Bible reference follows the Bible verse.

A plan for each week

Monday to Sunday

Monday	Learn the first verse for the week. There are only two verses to learn each week. That might seem rather slow to start with. But under this plan you end up memorizing one hundred verses each year. If you want to learn more than two verses a week you may do so, of course. But bear in mind is that some people find they give up memorizing verses altogether because it becomes too much for them.
Tuesday	Review your verses. This is explained on pages 16-17 under the topic *How do I review verses?*
Wednesday	Learn the second verse for the week. For each verse that you learn, write out the Bible verse on a card in the way that was explained in the previous two pages. Remember there are five things to place on each card. This book lists the one hundred verses for the first year, so all you have to do is to copy them.
Thursday	Review the two verses you have learned for this week.
Friday	Review your verses. This is explained on pages 16-17 under the topic *How do I review verses?*
Saturday	Review this week's verses again.
Sunday	Day off.

Strive for 100% accuracy

Settle for nothing less than 100% accuracy as you learn each verse. If you learn verses in even a slightly inaccurate way, you'll find it difficult in the future when you try to remember them.

I'm a slow learner

Don't worry if you do not have a photographic memory! The longer a verse takes to remember, the better because you will end up knowing it more thoroughly.

How to learn a verse

1. Read the whole verse. If possible, read it out aloud.
2. Pray to understand its meaning for you.
3. Break the verse into small parts. The punctuation in the verse often does this for you.
4. Then state the name of the topic, the first phrase of the Bible verse, and the Bible reference.
5. Add in the second phrase, and repeat the name of the topic, the first two phrases of the Bible verse and the Bible reference.
6. Keep adding in phrases until you have completed the verse.
7. Say by heart just the Bible verse three times.
8. Say by heart the topic, the Bible verse and the Bible reference.

Think about it from God's viewpoint

Did you know that God *wants* you to memorize his Word?

"These commandments that I give you today are to be upon your hearts." *Deuteronomy 6:6*

Your first week of memory verses

Here is your first week of verses.

Use *How to learn a verse* from page 13 when you learn your verses.

As this is your first week, and you have no verses to review, use your review days to check that these two verses are really part of your life. See what each verse means, and what it means for you. Think about whether the verses have changed your thinking, attitudes, or behavior in any way.

SIX KEYS 1/1/1
Loved by Jesus
"As the Father has loved me, so have I loved you. Now remain in my love." John 15:9

SIX KEYS 1/1/2
Loved by the Father
"For God so loved the world that he gave his one and only Son, that whoever believes in him shall not perish but have eternal life." John 3:16

More than merely memorizing words

Memorizing Scripture is more than memorizing words. While much time is spent on the mechanics of actually getting the verses into your brain, don't forget that this is just a small part of the course.

The lost art of meditating on Bible verses

If you have learned a Bible verse by heart, you can now meditate on it. You don't have to read it from your Bible. Since it is in your head, you can meditate on it wherever you are.

"But his delight is in the law of the LORD,
and on his law he meditates day and night."
Psalm 1:2

Meditating on the truths contained in Bible verses is not like day dreaming or any other kind of meditation. The Psalmist is specific – he says that he meditates on God's law.

How does this apply to me?

There is little point in remembering dozens of Bible verses and never asking yourself the question: How can this verse help me in my Christian life? One good way to do this is to see what there is in each verse that you can thank God for and then pray to God and thank him for that. Look for challenges, commands, and wonderful things about God himself in the verses you learn.

A habit for life

You are on the brink of acquiring a habit of learning Scripture. This could transform your Christian life. So be patient. Take the course seriously. And persevere.

"How do I review verses?"

Learning and forgetting
Most people find that by tomorrow they have forgotten the verse they learned today. They simply learn and forget.

Learning and remembering
The way to learn and remember is to review what you have learned. This means repeating today what you learned yesterday. It means repeating, repeating, repeating, day after day, after day, after day.

Review days: Tuesdays and Fridays

Here is a review plan. It is as important as the plan for memorizing verses.

On page 12, *A plan for each week*, you will see that Tuesdays and Fridays are set aside for reviewing. These are the days that you review the Bible verses which you have previously memorized.

Review plan for the year

Your second week's verses

Here are the two verses for your second week

You'll see that they continue the theme of love. Last week you memorized about how you are loved by Jesus and loved by God the Father. The first verse for this week focuses on how this love of God comes to us through the Holy Spirit. The second verse for this week centers on how Jesus loved us so much that he died for us.

As you progress with this course, look at each verse and before you memorize it. Pray about what it is saying to you personally.

SIX KEYS 1/2/1
Loved through the Spirit
And hope does not disappoint us, because God has poured out his love into our hearts by the Holy Spirit, whom he has given us. Romans 5:5

SIX KEYS 1/2/2
No greater love
"Greater love has no one than this, that he lay down his life for his friends." John 15:13

Plan for your second week of Scripture memory

Monday	Learn Romans 5:5.
Tuesday	Review your verses from week 1. Take the card 1/1/1 and look at the topic in the right hand corner: Loved by Jesus. Now say the verse and its reference. Check and double check that you are 100% accurate. Do the same with card 1/1/2. Now say the topics, Bible verse, and reference for both days.
Wednesday	Learn John 15:13.
Thursday	Review the two verses you have learned for this week.
Friday	Review your verses from week 1, as you did on Tuesday.
Saturday	Review this week's verses again.
Sunday	Day off.

Write out your verses

One good way to check that you have managed to remember your verses with complete accuracy is to write them out.
Write out the two Bible verses and their Bible references for the first week and check them carefully to see that they are perfect, word for word.

How to "picture" your verses

Make learning fun
Some people just love memorizing and need no incentives or helps at all. But most people think negatively about learning in this manner.

Make sure that however you go about learning these Bible verses that you follow a way that you enjoy and, if possible, find full of fun.

Hearing and "seeing"
Communications experts tell us that our sight gives us 83% of our total sensory input, our hearing gives us 11%, our sense of smell gives us 4%, and our sense of taste 2%. Obviously, our sight and hearing are our most important senses. The table below shows how much of their input we remember.

	After 3 hours	After 3 days
Hearing only	70%	10%
Sight only	72%	20%
Hearing and sight	85%	65%

This shows that the spoken word is more easily remembered if the hearer is able to visualize it and "see" what is being said.

Preach the words
Imagine that you are in the pulpit in the biggest church in the world. You are about to tell the packed church about these wonderful words from Scripture. You announce your text: "And hope does not disappoint us, because God has poured out his love into our hearts by the Holy Spirit, whom he has given us."

Say them slowly
Say the words out aloud.

From your pulpit say the words in a way that bring out their meaning.

Emphasize the words which you think are the key words. Introduce pauses, to allow your congregation to take in the meaning of the verse, phrase by phrase.

Romans 5:5

Your first verse for week 2 might be said in the following way.

> "And hope
> does not disappoint us,
> because God has poured out
> his love
> into our hearts
> by the Holy Spirit,
> whom he has given us."

Use your imagination

Think of yourself reading this letter for the first time to the early Christians in Rome, huddled together in a Christian's home, listening eagerly to every word from the letter of the famous theologian and missionary, Paul: "And hope does not disappoint us, because God has poured out his love into our hearts by the Holy Spirit, whom he has given us."

Your third week's verses

Here are your verses for your third week. Observe what they are about before you learn them.

SIX KEYS 1/3/1	SIX KEYS 1/3/2
God is love	No separation from love
And so we know and rely on the love God has for us. God is love. Whoever lives in love lives in God, and God in him. 1 John 4:16	. . . neither height nor depth, nor anything else in all creation, will be able to separate us from the love of God that is in Christ Jesus our Lord. Romans 8:39

Monday to Sunday

Monday	Learn 1 John 4:16.
Tuesday	The verses to review this week are the verses from weeks 1 and 2. On pages 16–17, under the table *Review plan for the year*, you will see which verses you have to review each week.
Wednesday	Learn Romans 8:39.
Thursday	Review the two verses you have learned for this week.
Friday	Repeat what you did on Tuesday.
Saturday	Review this week's two verses again.
Sunday	Day off.

Memory aid

Each theme has been given a memory aid, and they are noted on the pull out section at the end of the book. Unsurprisingly, the memory aid for the first three weeks of verses is: KEY.

Themes
The one hundred verses to be learned have been divided into twelve themes:

1 Six keys to the Christian life

2 God's plan of salvation

3 Jesus' six "I am's"

4 The Holy Spirit at work

5 Bible promises

6 Jesus and his cross

7 How can I be sure that I am a Christian?

8 How can I grow as a Christian?

9 Witnessing for Jesus

10 Words of comfort

11 Psalm 23

12 1 Corinthians 13

Handy hints about your memory

Do you have a bad memory?

Most of us think that we do have a bad memory. We often find it hard to remember anything longer than a short sentence.

But this is not because we have a bad memory. It is because we have an untrained memory. This course will help train your memory.

Review

As a piano teacher says, "Practice, practice, practice," so this Scripture memory course says, "Review, review, review."

One of the keys to successful memory work is reviewing what you have learned. Don't skip the reviewing this course gives you. It is the most permanent way of learning. Look forward to reviewing – it is the key to successfully remembering Scripture.

If you forget a word

When you forget a word in a Bible verse, repeat the phrase that contains the word three times. Then say the whole verse three times.

Do you have a patient friend?

If so, say your verses to him or her.

Listen to the verse

Record the verse on a cassette. Start with the topic, then the verse and its reference.

You could do this for all one hundred verses. How surprised people would be if they knew what you were listening to on your Walkman!

"Practice makes perfect"

"Practice makes perfect" is a phrase used by memory teaching experts. All they are saying is: put into practice what you have learned. For a Christian who is learning Bible verses, there could be no better advice.

As Christians, we know that we are meant to live out in our lives what we discover in the Bible. As we do this, it also helps us remember particular Bible verses.

Reading, hearing, speaking

When you link reading, hearing, and speaking you are much more likely to remember what you learn. When you make use of your Bible knowledge, you are reinforcing the learning process.

- So read the verses you are learning.
- Listen to the verses you are learning by saying them aloud or listening to a cassette.
- "Speak" the Bible verses as you put into practice the verses you are learning, by talking about them with others, or meditating on them in your heart.

Weeks 4–6: God's plan of salvation

GOD'S PLAN OF SALVATION	GOD'S PLAN OF SALVATION	GOD'S PLAN OF SALVATION
1/4/1	1/4/2	1/5/1
All are lost	All have sinned	Sin ends in death
We all, like sheep, have gone astray, each of us has turned to his own way; and the LORD has laid on him the iniquity of us all. Isaiah 53:6	. . . for all have sinned and fall short of the glory of God. Romans 3:23	For the wages of sin is death, but the gift of God is eternal life in Christ Jesus our Lord. Romans 6:23

GOD'S PLAN OF SALVATION	GOD'S PLAN OF SALVATION	GOD'S PLAN OF SALVATION
1/5/2	1/6/1	1/6/2
Jesus died to bring you to God	Jesus took your sins	Come in, Lord Jesus
For Christ died for sins once for all, the righteous for the unrighteous, to bring you to God. He was put to death in the body but made alive by the Spirit. 1 Peter 3:18	He himself bore our sins in his body on the tree, so that we might die to sins and live for righteousness; by his wounds you have been healed. 1 Peter 2:24	"Here I am! I stand at the door and knock. If anyone hears my voice and opens the door, I will come in and eat with him, and he with me." Revelation 3:20

There are six verses in this second theme of *God's plan of salvation*. They are set out for you to learn over the next three weeks.

The bridge illustration

These verses are often linked to the bridge illustration as a way of helping someone to see what Jesus did on the cross.

People

On the left hand side of the bridge are people. They depict the plight that everyone is in.

The first three verses of *God's plan of salvation* spell out the spiritual condition of humankind: all have sinned, all are lost, and sin ends in death.

The cross

The central part of the bridge shows the cross of Jesus. The purpose of Jesus' death is stated in the next two verses: Jesus died to bring you to God, and Jesus died for your sins.

God

On the right hand side of the illustration is God. We come to God by making the last verse we are learning in this theme into a prayer. We ask the Lord Jesus to come into our lives in response to his knocking on the door of our lives.

Weeks 7–9: Six "I am's" of Jesus

SIX "I AM'S" OF JESUS 1/7/1
Bread
Then Jesus declared, "I am the bread of life. He who comes to me will never go hungry, and he who believes in me will never be thirsty." John 6:35

SIX "I AM'S" OF JESUS 1/7/2
Light
When Jesus spoke again to the people he said, "I am the light of the world. Whoever follows me will never walk in darkness, but will have the light of life." John 8:12

SIX "I AM'S" OF JESUS 1/8/1
Gate
"I am the gate; whoever enters through me will be saved. He will come in and go out, and find pasture." John 10:9

SIX "I AM'S" OF JESUS 1/8/2
Good Shepherd
"I am the good shepherd. The good shepherd lays down his life for the sheep." John 10:11

SIX "I AM'S" OF JESUS 1/9/1
Resurrection and life
Jesus said to her, "I am the resurrection and the life. He who believes in me will live, even though he dies." John 11:25

SIX "I AM'S" OF JESUS 1/9/2
Way, Truth, Life
Jesus answered, "I am the way and the truth and the life. No one comes to the Father except through me." John 14:6

28

John's Gospel

One of the most helpful ways to recall who Jesus is, is to mull over what he said about himself. In John's Gospel he explains who he is by using the words, "I am."

More and more verses

By the end of this theme, you will have learned eighteen verses. You may be wondering how you are going to remember them all, especially as you are adding to them at the rate of two a week.

Pull-out chart

The pull-out chart at the end of this book has a number of lists.

1. It lists the fifty-two weeks of the year.
2. It lists the Bible references of the one hundred Bible verses
3. It lists the topic for each of the Bible verses
4. It lists the twelve themes for the whole year

Rocket

On the right hand side is a rocket. This links all the themes as an aid to your memory. It uses an abbreviation or symbol for each theme, and depicts this inside a room in the space ship. The idea is to make it easy to remember that your verses start with a key, then follow a plan. The six "I am's" are depicted by a giant placard with the words "I am" on it.

"What do I do when I want to give up?"

This is quite normal

Most people find that they go through a time, or many times, when they feel like giving up learning Bible verses.

A spiritual activity

Memorizing Scripture, if engaged in properly, launches you into a spiritual battle. Satan does not want you to stick with it to the end. He will stop at nothing to keep you from growing closer and closer to Jesus.

Satan will not be happy that you are learning Bible verses.

> "Be self-controlled and alert. Your enemy the devil prowls around like a roaring lion looking for someone to devour." *1 Peter 5:8*

So what are we to do? How do we respond? Peter continues:

> "Resist him, standing firm in the faith, because you know that your brothers throughout the world are undergoing the same kind of sufferings." *1 Peter 5:9*

Learning difficulties

If one particular verse seems difficult to learn, try this idea.

Go back to reading the verse from your card instead of attempting to recite it from memory.

Read it aloud "word by word" and "syllable by syllable." Use 1 Peter 3:18: "For Christ died for sins once for all, the righteous for the unrighteous, to bring you to God. He was put to death in the body but made alive by the Spirit." Read it slowly like this:

For – Christ – died – for – sins – once – for – all, – the – right-eous – for – the – un-right-eous, – to – bring – you – to – God. – He – was – put – to – death – in – the – bo-dy – but – made – a-live – by – the – Spir-it.

Say it like this over and over again until you feel that you really know it.

So, how much do you want to grow in your Christian life?

Jesus said, "Blessed are those who hunger and thirst for righteousness." He went on to add this promise, "'for they will be filled.'" *Matthew 5:6*

Memorizing Scripture will help you become a stronger Christian if you are prayerful about it. So the first thing to do when you feel like giving up is to pray to God about how you feel.

Have you thought of memorizing Scripture with a friend?

If you think that would help, find a friend to work with you in memorizing Scripture.

It is also a good idea to ask at least one other Christian to pray for you as you set out to memorize Scripture.

Week 10: Review, review, review

No new verses

This week there are no new verses to learn. There are no verses to review. It's a time to reflect on how you are progressing.

Examination time

If you want to see how well you are doing, give yourself this simple test.

Write out all your verses for weeks 1–8 at one sitting. You should include the Bible references. Don't worry if you cannot remember all the topics. But write them down as you come to each verse, even if you have to look them up.

Then check each verse and reference carefully. Don't worry about any mistakes you may have made. Just relearn the verse.

Do this once on Monday and each day of the week until you know it perfectly, word for word.

"Pray in" a verse a day

Once you have managed to write out all your verses with 100% accuracy, select one verse a day from those you have learned and spend a little time "praying in" its message so that your heart is warmed by what it says.

You may say that you already spent time "praying in" each verse when you first learned it. But you may be surprised at how many new layers of meaning God unfolds in each verse as you learn more about yourself and about God.

> "'Were not our hearts burning within us while [Jesus] talked with us on the road and opened the Scriptures to us?'"
> *Luke 24:32*

When to review

In addition to the set times when you review your verses, think about how you can review them at other times. If you carry your Bible memory verse cards with you in your pocket, wallet, or purse, you may find some spare time in the day when you can review them.

Seven years' worth of waiting in lines

Someone has figured out that most of us spend up to seven years of our lives waiting in lines. These may be ideal moments for you to review your verses.

Go over in your mind one set of verses from one of the themes. Go through all the verses at one time. Then hold one verse at a time in your mind and meditate on it. See what it is saying at that moment.

Awake at night

If you wake up in the night, focus on one of your most recently learned verses and repeat it, "feeding" on its spiritual content.

> "I will praise the LORD who counsels me; even at night my heart instructs me." *Psalm 16:7*

Weeks 11–15: The Holy Spirit at work

THE HOLY SPIRIT	1/11/1

Helping you understand

We have not received the spirit of the world but the Spirit who is from God, that we may understand what God has freely given us.
1 Corinthians 2:12

THE HOLY SPIRIT	1/11/2

Fellowship

May the grace of the Lord Jesus Christ, and the love of God, and the fellowship of the Holy Spirit be with you all.
2 Corinthians 13:14

THE HOLY SPIRIT	1/12/1

Lives in you

Don't you know that you yourselves are God's temple and that God's Spirit lives in you?
1 Corinthians 3:16

THE HOLY SPIRIT	1/12/2

Brings joy

For the kingdom of God is not a matter of eating and drinking, but of righteousness, peace and joy in the Holy Spirit.
Romans 14:17

There are ten verses to learn under this new theme *The Holy Spirit at work*.

1 Corinthians 2:12	Helping you understand
2 Corinthians 13:14	Fellowship
1 Corinthians 3:16	Lives in you
Romans 14:17	Brings joy
Galatians 5:25	Keep in step with
Romans 8:26	Helps in prayer
1 John 4:13	God's gift
John 14:16	With you forever
Ephesians 5:18	Be filled
John 14:26	Teaches you

34

Remembering the topics

As with all the other verses, each of these ten verses about the Holy Spirit has been given a topic.

When reviewing verses, many people find it helpful to have a way of remembering which order they come in. For these verses a simple acrostic on the words HOLY SPIRIT has been devised. If you find it helpful, it is easy to use.

THE HOLY SPIRIT 1/13/1 Keep in step with Since we live by the Spirit, let us keep in step with the Spirit. Galatians 5:25	**THE HOLY SPIRIT** 1/13/2 Helps in prayer In the same way, the Spirit helps us in our weakness. We do not know what we ought to pray for, but the Spirit himself intercedes for us with groans that words cannot express. Romans 8:26	**THE HOLY SPIRIT** 1/14/1 God's gift We know that we live in him and he in us, because he has given us of his Spirit. 1 John 4:13
THE HOLY SPIRIT 1/14/2 With you for ever "And I will ask the Father, and he will give you another Counselor to be with you forever." John 14:16	**THE HOLY SPIRIT** 1/15/1 Be filled Do not get drunk on wine, which leads to debauchery. Instead, be filled with the Spirit. Ephesians 5:18	**THE HOLY SPIRIT** 1/15/2 Teaches you "But the Counselor, the Holy Spirit, whom the Father will send in my name, will teach you all things and will remind you of everything I have said to you." John 14:26

All you have to do is to go through the letters making up the word HOLY SPIRIT trying to remember the word or words which relate to each letter.

HOLY SPIRIT acrostic

Helping you understand
Fell**O**wship
Lives in you
Brings jo**Y**
Keep in **S**tep with
Helps in **P**rayer
God's g**I**ft
With you foreve**R**
Be f**I**lled
Teaches you

More handy hints

We remember what we understand

If you don't understand any of the verses you are learning, look them up in a Bible commentary or ask somebody to explain them to you.

> "But the one who received the seed that fell on good soil is the man who hears the word and understands it. He produces a crop, yielding a hundred, sixty or thirty times what was sown."
> *Matthew 13:23*

Your mind accepts and remembers what it understands but tends to put up a barrier against remembering what it is unable to grasp or comprehend.

We focus on what we think is relevant

When people go shopping, even just window-shopping, they only take time to stop and look at what they are interested in.

If you believe that these Bible verses can transform your life, and if you strongly desire to be a more faithful disciple of Jesus, you will not need anyone to point out the value of memorizing Scripture. You will never stop wanting to absorb into your life more and more of God's Word.

How Scripture memory is relevant to you

Memorizing Scripture helps you to:

- **overcome worry.**

  "Great peace have they who love your law, and nothing can make them stumble."
  Psalm 119:165

- **defeat sin.**

  The Psalmist wrote:

  "I have hidden your word in my heart that I might not sin against you." *Psalm 119:11*

  "In your battle against Satan and sin you now have God's word tucked in your heart. Paul calls it "the sword of the Spirit, which is the word of God."
  Ephesians 6:17

Slow and steady wins the race

A whole number of things memorized at great speed are less likely to be remembered than a few things learned slowly.

Who can climb a pyramid?

According to an eastern proverb, there are only two creatures that can surmount the pyramids: the eagle and the snail.

Perseverence is a great Christian virtue and it is hard to overvalue its importance in memory work.

"'You have persevered and have endured hardships for my name, and have not grown weary.'" *Revelation 2:3*

Weeks 16–21: Bible promises

BIBLE PROMISES 1/16/1
Answered prayer
"Again, I tell you that if two of you on earth agree about anything you ask for, it will be done for you by my Father in heaven." Matthew 18:19

BIBLE PROMISES 1/16/2
Burdened people
"Come to me, all you who are weary and burdened, and I will give you rest." Matthew 11:28

BIBLE PROMISES 1/17/1
Christ's peace
"Peace I leave with you; my peace I give you. I do not give to you as the world gives. Do not let your hearts be troubled and do not be afraid." John 14:27

BIBLE PROMISES 1/17/2
Death is not the end
By his power God raised the Lord from the dead, and he will raise us also. 1 Corinthians 6:14

BIBLE PROMISES 1/18/1
Everlasting covenant
". . . I will make an everlasting covenant with them: I will never stop doing good to them, and I will inspire them to fear me, so that they will never turn away from me." Jeremiah 32:40

BIBLE PROMISES 1/18/2
Forgiveness
As far as the east is from the west, so far has he removed our transgressions from us. Psalm 103:12

This theme about Bible promises is the longest so far and has twelve verses in it.

Promise boxes

In Victorian times some Christians would pass around a promise box on Sunday afternoons. It looked a little like a box of chocolates. Instead of chocolates it was filled with tiny scrolls with a promise from the Bible written on each scroll. People passed around the promise box and everyone took a scroll and treated it as their promise from God for the week.

A promise box has been used as a way to help you remember the twelve verses in this theme, each of which starts with a consecutive letter of the alphabet.

BIBLE PROMISES 1/19/1	BIBLE PROMISES 1/19/2	BIBLE PROMISES 1/20/1
God's presence	Heart and spirit	Instruction
"Have I not commanded you? Be strong and courageous. Do not be terrified; do not be discouraged, for the LORD your God will be with you wherever you go." Joshua 1:9	"I will give you a new heart and put a new spirit in you; I will remove from you your heart of stone and give you a heart of flesh." Ezekiel 36:26	I will instruct you and teach you in the way you should go; I will counsel you and watch over you. Psalm 32:8

BIBLE PROMISES 1/20/2	BIBLE PROMISES 1/21/1	BIBLE PROMISES 1/21/2
Jesus' resurrection	Knowledge of God	Life from the Spirit
. . . because he was teaching his disciples. He said to them, "The Son of Man is going to be betrayed into the hands of men. They will kill him, and after three days he will rise." Mark 9:31	His divine power has given us everything we need for life and godliness through our knowledge of him who called us by his own glory and goodness. 2 Peter 1:3	"The Spirit gives life; the flesh counts for nothing. The words I have spoken to you are spirit and they are life." John 6:63

39

A–B–C–D–E–F–G–H–I–J–K–L

How to turn memorizing verses into Bible studies

Look at the context

Look up a verse in your Bible you have memorized and read the verses that surround it.

Use, for example, the last verse you have learned: Life from the Spirit. "'The Spirit gives life; the flesh counts for nothing. The words I have spoken to you are spirit and they are life.'"
John 6:63

Start by reading the paragraph in which the verse occurs, that is, John 6:61-65. Then look at the section from which the paragraph comes. The heading to the section given by *The New International Version* is "Many Disciples Desert Jesus." So John 6:63 is given by Jesus as an antidote to disciples who were grumbling and saying of Jesus' words, "'This is a hard teaching,'" *(John 6:60)*.

When you understand this background to the verse, you can see why Jesus said these words and appreciate just how important they are.

Ask questions about the verse

Is there a command, a promise, or a warning – or all three – in the verse?

Link up verses

The following list has all one hundred Bible verses used in this course. The verses are followed by the number of the week in which they appear.

Start by reading the chapters in the Bible where a number of Bible verses are used in different weeks. There are five verses from John chapter 14, for example, where each verse comes in a different week. Read all of John chapter 14, and then see how the four verses in the different weeks are used.

Joshua		Mark		Romans		2 Corinthians		1 Peter	
1:9	19	9:31	20	3:23	4	1:3	41	2:24	6
				5:1	23	5:14	27	3:15	40
Psalm		John		5:5	2	5:17	30	3:18	5
23:1	43	3:16	1	5:8	26	13:14	11	5:7	41
23:2	43	5:24	31	6:23	5				
23:3	44	6:35	7	8:1	31	Galatians		2 Peter	
23:4	44	6:37	32	8:26	13	2:20	28	1:3	21
23:5	45	6:63	21	8:39	3	5:25	13		
23:6	45	8:12	7	12:1	33			1 John	
27:5	42	10:9	8	14:17	12	Ephesians		1:9	24
32:8	20	10:11	8			1:7	24	2:2	29
103:12	18	10:29	32	1 Corinthians		2:14	22	3:18	33
119:9	36	11:25	9	2:12	11	2:16	23	4:10	26
		14:6	9	3:16	12	5:2	27	4:13	14
Isaiah		14:16	14	6:14	17	5:3	36	4:16	3
41:10	35	14:21	35	12:31	46	5:18	15	5:13	30
53:6	4	14:26	15	13:1	46				
		14:27	17	13:2	47	Colossians		Revelation	
Jeremiah		15:7	34	13:3	47	1:20	22	3:20	6
32:40	18	15:9	1	13:4	48			21:4	42
		15:13	2	13:5	48	Hebrews			
Ezekiel				13:6	49	9:26	28		
36:26	19	Acts		13:7	49	10:14	29		
		5:31	25	13:8	50	11:6	37		
Matthew		10:43	25	13:9	50				
4:19	39			13:10	51	James			
5:16	39			13:11	51	4:7	37		
11:28	16			13:12	52				
18:19	16			13:13	52				
18:20	34								
28:19	40								

41

Weeks 22–29: Jesus and his cross

JESUS AND HIS CROSS 1/22/1
Peace through Christ's death

And through him to reconcile to himself all things, whether things on earth or things in heaven, by making peace through his blood, shed on the cross.
Colossians 1:20

JESUS AND HIS CROSS 1/22/2
Jesus is our peace

For he himself is our peace, who has made the two one and has destroyed the barrier, the dividing wall of hostility.
Ephesians 2:14

JESUS AND HIS CROSS 1/23/1
Peace in place of hostility

. . . and in this one body to reconcile both of them to God through the cross, by which he put to death their hostility.
Ephesians 2:16

JESUS AND HIS CROSS 1/23/2
Peace with God

Therefore, since we have been justified through faith, we have peace with God through our Lord Jesus Christ.
Romans 5:1

JESUS AND HIS CROSS 1/24/1
Forgiveness and cleansing

If we confess our sins, he is faithful and just and will forgive us our sins and purify us from all unrighteousness.
1 John 1:9

JESUS AND HIS CROSS 1/24/2
Forgiveness and redemption

In him we have redemption through his blood, the forgiveness of sins, in accordance with the riches of God's grace.
Ephesians 1:7

JESUS AND HIS CROSS 1/25/1
Forgiveness and belief

"All the prophets testify about him that everyone who believes in him receives forgiveness of sins through his name."
Acts 10:43

JESUS AND HIS CROSS 1/25/2
Forgiveness and repentance

"God exalted him to his own right hand as Prince and Savior that he might give repentance and forgiveness of sins to Israel."
Acts 5:31

JESUS AND HIS CROSS 1/26/1
Love for sinners

But God demonstrates his own love for us in this: While we were still sinners, Christ died for us.
Romans 5:8

JESUS AND HIS CROSS 1/26/2
Love and expiation
for sins

This is love: not that
we loved God, but that
he loved us and sent
his Son as an atoning
sacrifice for our
sins.
1 John 4:10

JESUS AND HIS CROSS 1/27/1
Compelled by Christ's
love

For Christ's love
compels us, because
we are convinced that
one died for all, and
therefore all died.
2 Corinthians 5:14

JESUS AND HIS CROSS 1/27/2
Love and Jesus giving
himself

. . . and live a life of
love, just as Christ
loved us and gave
himself up for us as a
fragrant offering
and sacrifice to God.
Ephesians 5:2

JESUS AND HIS CROSS 1/28/1
Sacrifice and love

I have been crucified
with Christ and I no
longer live, but
Christ lives in me.
The life I live in the
body, I live by faith in
the Son of God, who
loved me and gave
himself for me.
Galatians 2:20

JESUS AND HIS CROSS 1/28/2
The sacrifice of
Jesus himself
Then Christ would have
had to suffer many
times since the
creation of the world.
But now he has
appeared once for all at
the end of the ages to
do away with sin by the
sacrifice of himself.
Hebrews 7:26

JESUS AND HIS CROSS 1/29/1
Jesus' one sacrifice

. . . because by one
sacrifice he has made
perfect for ever
those who are being
made holy.
Hebrews 10:14

43

JESUS AND HIS CROSS 1/29/2
Sacrifice for our
sins

He is the atoning
sacrifice for our
sins, and not only for
ours but also for the
sins of the whole
world.
1 John 2:2

Visualizing
One way of picturing these sixteen verses
about Jesus and his cross is to divide
them into four and link each set of four
to the four points of the cross. Label
these points, WIDTH, LENGTH,
HEIGHT, and DEPTH, following
Paul's verse about the love of Jesus: ". . .
to grasp how wide and long and high and
deep is the love of Christ . . ."
Ephesians 3:18

"I'm slipping. What do I do now?"

Don't give up!

There may be overwhelming personal reasons, like illness or problems at home or work, that have made it impossible for you to stay on track.

Don't worry if you have been forced to stop. Give it a break and return to it later on.

The sin problem

This may not be the reason why you stopped, but it does stop some people. It's been said that "The Bible will keep you from sin or sin will keep you from the Bible." Some people stop memorizing Scripture because one sin, or a number of sins, have overwhelmed their lives.

It may seem like the end of the world, or at least the end of your Christian life, but it need not be. It looked like the end for King David when he committed adultery with Bathsheba and arranged for her husband Uriah to be killed in battle. But God restored David.

The remedy

Read passages like 1 John 1:5-10, confess your sin, make right with God whatever needs to be made right, and carry on in your Christian life.

"This is the message we have heard from him and declare to you: God is light; in him there is no darkness at all. If we claim to have fellowship with him yet walk in the darkness, we lie and do not live by the truth. But if we walk in the light, as he is in the light, we have fellowship with one another, and the blood of Jesus, his Son, purifies us from all sin. If we claim to be without sin, we deceive ourselves and the truth is not in us. If we confess our sins, he is faithful and just and will forgive us our sins and purify us from all unrighteousness. If we claim we have not sinned, we make him out to be a liar and his word has no place in our lives."
1 John 1:5-10

Remember some of the reasons for memorizing Scripture

God's word in our hearts keeps our feet from slipping.	*Read Psalm 37:28-31*
It drives Satan away when he is tempting us, as Jesus knew.	*Read Matthew 4:1-11*
Knowing the word of God was, for the psalmist, a key to purity.	*Read Psalm 119:9-11*
The word is the sword to defeat the devil's plots to bring us down.	*Read Ephesians 6:13-18*

I feel bored

Ask God to restore the joy of your salvation.

"Restore to me the joy of your salvation." *Psalm 51:12*

No Christian escapes the need for forgiveness

"If you, O LORD, kept a record of sins, O LORD, who could stand? But with you there is forgiveness; therefore you are feared." *Psalm 130:3-4*

Weeks 30–32: "How can I be sure that I am a Christian?"

HOW CAN I BE SURE? 1/30/1 From death to life Therefore, if anyone is in Christ he is a new creation; the old has gone, the new has come! 2 Corinthians 5:17	**HOW CAN I BE SURE? 1/30/2** Eternal life I write these things to you who believe in the name of the Son of God so that you may know that you have eternal life. 1 John 5:13	**HOW CAN I BE SURE? 1/31/1** Promised "I tell you the truth, whoever hears my word and believes him who sent me has eternal life and will not be condemned; he has crossed over from death to life." John 5:24
HOW CAN I BE SURE? 1/31/2 God's call Therefore, there is now no condemnation for those who are in Christ Jesus. Romans 8:1	**HOW CAN I BE SURE? 1/32/1** Welcomed "All the Father gives me will come to me, and whoever comes to me I will never drive away." John 6:37	**HOW CAN I BE SURE? 1/32/2** Safe "My Father, who has given them to me, is greater than all; no one can snatch them out of my Father's hand." John 10:29

One of the most debilitating things that can happen to Christians is when they think that they may not be Christians after all. They may entertain grave doubts that Jesus ever came into the their lives or whether he is still with them.

These six arrows are ideal for shooting at the target of doubt, as they will each score a bull's-eye.

Weeks 33–37: "How can I grow as a Christian?"

HOW CAN I GROW? 1/33/1
Dedication

Therefore, I urge you, brothers, in view of God's mercy, to offer your bodies as living sacrifices, holy and pleasing to God — this is your spiritual act of worship.
Romans 12:1

HOW CAN I GROW? 1/33/2
Action

Dear children, let us not love with words or tongue but with actions and in truth.
1 John 3:18

HOW CAN I GROW? 1/34/1
With others

"For where two or three come together in my name, there am I with them."
Matthew 18:20

HOW CAN I GROW? 1/34/2
Pray

"If you remain in me and my words remain in you, ask whatever you wish, and it will be given you."
John 15:7

HOW CAN I GROW? 1/35/1
Obey

"Whoever has my commands and obeys them, he is the one who loves me. He who loves me will be loved by my Father, and I too will love him and show myself to him."
John 14:21

HOW CAN I GROW? 1/35/2
Strength

"So do not fear, for I am with you; do not be dismayed, for I am your God. I will strengthen you and help you; I will uphold you with my righteous right hand."
Isaiah 41:10

Birth – growth

Birth should lead to growth in our physical lives. It is exactly the same in our spiritual lives. Peter speaks to us about growth in this verse where the word milk stands for God's Word.

"Like newborn babies, crave pure spiritual milk, so that by it you may grow up in your salvation, now that you have tasted that the Lord is good." *1 Peter 2:2-3*

HOW CAN I GROW? 1/36/1
Purity

But among you there must be not even a hint of sexual immorality, or of any kind of impurity, or of greed, because these are improper for God's holy people.
Ephesians 5:3

HOW CAN I GROW? 1/36/2
Bible

How can a young man keep his way pure? By living according to your word.
Psalm 119:9

HOW CAN I GROW? 1/37/1
Resist

Submit yourselves, then, to God. Resist the devil, and he will flee from you.
James 4:7

HOW CAN I GROW? 1/37/2
Faith

And without faith it is impossible to please God, because anyone who comes to him must believe that he exists and that he rewards those who earnestly seek him.
Hebrews 11:6

Week 38: Review, review, review

Learning a verse

It has been said that a Bible verse is not really memorized until you have reviewed it _____ times. How many times do you think it is necessary to review a verse before you are certain that you will never forget it? Six times, twenty-six times, eighty-six times? Well, the answer many writers on this topic give is *one hundred* times.

So, you should never think of reviewing as a waste of time. Every time you review a verse, you are helping your memory.

I can't keep up

It really does not matter how many verses you learn in a year. What matters is that the verses that you do learn make an impact on your spiritual growth. So, if you prefer to learn one verse a week, that's fine. Just adapt this course to suit what suits you best.

A good tip is not to learn more verses until you have reviewed the ones you have already learned. You need to be totally confident that you know them with 100% accuracy. This may mean that you will need to spend an extra week reviewing. If that is necessary, fine.

As you sleep, as you wake up

Try reviewing your verses as you go to sleep at night.

- Start with the verse you have most recently learned.
- The next night try to review all the verses in the theme you are currently learning.
- The next night review the previous theme.
- The next night review the theme before that, and take one theme a night until you reach the first theme.
- The next night review two themes. Keep on doing this until you are able to review all your Bible verses at one time!
- Try the same thing as you wake up.

Build up to this very slowly. Take your time.

Day and night

"Blessed is the man who does not walk in the counsel of the wicked or stand in the way of sinners or sit in the seat of mockers. But his delight is in the law of the LORD, and on his law he meditates day and night. He is like a tree planted by streams of water, which yields its fruit in season and whose leaf does not wither. Whatever he does prospers." *Psalm 1:1-3*

More reasons for memorizing Scripture

Keep your goal in sight

One way to stop yourself from being deflected from a lifetime habit of memorizing Scripture is to keep focused on why you are doing this. It is much easier to learn something if you are totally convinced of its vital importance.

Psalm 119

This is the longest psalm and the longest chapter in the Bible. Nearly all of its 176 verses tell us something about God's Word. It is divided into twenty-two sections, one for each letter of the Hebrew alphabet.

Read one eight-verse section a day and find the seven different words the psalmist uses for God's Word.

The importance of knowing and following God's Word is provided here in great detail. It will stimulate you to keep moving ahead with your own memorization of Scripture.

Word, decrees, promises

- "Direct my footsteps according to your word; let no sin rule over me." *Psalm 119:133*
- "Make your face shine upon your servant and teach me your decrees." *Psalm 119:135*
- "My eyes stay open through the watches of the night, that I may meditate on your promises." *Psalm 119:148*

The encouragement of the Scriptures

The writers of the New Testament often said how much we can learn from the Old Testament.

"For everything that was written in the past was written to teach us, so that through endurance and the encouragement of the Scriptures we might have hope." *Romans 15:4*

Memorize for others

Asking God to build you up in your Christian life is never a selfish prayer. Others will always benefit.

By memorizing the Bible verses suggested for the next two weeks – on pages 54-55 "Witnessing for Jesus" – you will feel better equipped to talk about Jesus with other people.

"Ezra had devoted himself to the study . . ."

"For Ezra had devoted himself to the study and observance of the Law of the LORD, and to teaching its decrees and laws in Israel." *Ezra 7:10*

"Do your best . . ."

"Do your best to present yourself to God as one approved, a workman who does not need to be ashamed and who correctly handles the word of truth." *2 Timothy 2:15*

Weeks 39–40: Witnessing for Jesus

WITNESSING FOR JESUS
1/39/1
Fishing for Jesus

"Come, follow me,"
Jesus said, "and I
will make you fishers
of men."
Matthew 4:19

WITNESSING FOR JESUS
1/39/2
Shine

"In the same way, let
your light shine
before men, that
they may see your
good deeds and praise
your Father in
heaven."
Matthew 5:16

WITNESSING FOR JESUS
1/40/1
Give a reason
But in your hearts set
apart Christ as Lord.
Always be prepared to
give an answer to
everyone who asks you
to give the reason for
the hope that you have.
But do this with
gentleness and
respect. 1 Peter 3:15

WITNESSING FOR JESUS
1/40/2
make disciples

"Therefore go and
make disciples of all
nations, baptizing
them in the name of
the Father and of the
Son and of the Holy
Spirit."
Matthew 28:19

The pull-down chart
The pull-down chart at
the end of the book
suggests that a way to
remember the theme
"Witnessing for Jesus"
is the symbol of a
fishing rod depicted by
a scene of fish being
caught.

Remembering the order

The four topics under this theme with their verses are:

Matthew 4:19	Fishing for Jesus
Matthew 5:16	Shine
1 Peter 3:15	Give a reason
Matthew 28:19	Make disciples

When it comes to reviewing verses, especially when you are doing this in your head and are not able to look at your memory cards, it is helpful to be able to remember the order in which the topics come for each theme.

On pages 34–35, the idea of an acrostic on the words HOLY SPIRIT was suggested for memorizing the order of the ten topics under the theme of the Holy Spirit

Do It Yourself

The best memory aids are the ones you make up yourself. So devise a way to remember the order of these four topics on the theme Witnessing for Jesus. Jot it down on the back of memory card 1/39/1 in case you forget it.

Weeks 41–42: Words of comfort

....

WORDS OF COMFORT 1/41/1
God of comfort

Praise be to the God
and Father of our
Lord Jesus Christ,
the Father of
compassion and the
God of all comfort.
2 Corinthians 1:3

WORDS OF COMFORT 1/41/2
God cares

Cast all your anxiety
on him because he
cares for you.
1 Peter 5:7

WORDS OF COMFORT 1/42/2
Safety

For in the day of
trouble he will keep
me safe in his
dwelling; he will hide
me in the shelter of
his tabernacle and set
me high upon a rock.
Psalm 27:5

WORDS OF COMFORT 1/42/2
No crying

"He will wipe every
tear from their
eyes. There will be no
more death or
mourning or crying or
pain, for the old
order of things has
passed away."
Revelation 21:4

Thermometer
On the pull-out chart a thermometer is the
symbol used to remember the theme "Words
of comfort."

Hospital bed
A hospital bed is suggested as the
memory aid. There are four bottles at the
bedside. These labeled bottles have the
following names on them:
• God of comfort
• God cares
• Safety
• No crying

The ministry of comfort
All Christians can bring God's comfort
to people every day.
  "Rejoice with those who rejoice; mourn
  with those who mourn." *Romans 12:15*

56

GOD
OF
COMFORT

How to learn longer passages of Scripture

1. Select your chapter
Once you've chosen a chapter, don't change it.

2. Familiarize yourself with the whole chapter
Read the chapter from start to finish many times – ten times would not be too many – before you start memorizing even the first verse.

3. Understand the chapter
You may want to read a commentary or two about the chapter to help you understand it.

4. Do a mini Bible study on the chapter
Write down the following things about it:
• its main theme
• its key word or words
• its main sections

5. Write the chapter out
Copy the whole chapter onto your Bible memory cards. Put one verse only on each card. Use the name of the Bible book and its chapter as the theme.

   Don't worry about putting a topic on the cards as you write out the chapter. You can do this as you come to learn each verse. If you become completely stuck about what word or words to use for a topic, chose one from the verse itself.

Writing out verses

If you are learning poetry-style verses from the Psalms, it is usually helpful to follow the style that your Bible uses. But you may find that a passage like Romans 8:38-39 is easier to remember if you do not simply copy it out as run-on words, as printed in your Bible.

"For I am convinced that neither death nor life, neither angels nor demons, neither the present nor the future, nor any powers, neither height nor depth, nor anything else in all creation, will be able to separate us from the love of God that is in Christ Jesus our Lord."
Romans 8:38-39

Use your imagination
"For I am convinced that
neither death nor life,
neither angels nor demons,
neither the present nor the future,
nor any powers,
neither height nor depth,
nor anything else in all creation,
will be able to separate us
    from the love of God
        that is in Christ Jesus our Lord."
Romans 8:38-39

Weeks 43–45: Psalm 23

PSALM 23 1/43/1 Shepherd The LORD is my shepherd, I shall not be in want. Psalm 23:1	**PSALM 23** 1/43/2 Pasture He makes me lie down in green pastures, he leads me beside quiet waters, Psalm 23:2	**PSALM 23** 1/44/1 Restores he restores my soul. He guides me in paths of righteousness for his name's sake. Psalm 23:3
PSALM 23 1/44/2 Comfort Even though I walk through the valley of the shadow of death, I will fear no evil, for you are with me; your rod and your staff, they comfort me. Psalm 23:4	**PSALM 23** 1/45/1 Anointed You prepare a table before me in the presence of my enemies. You anoint my head with oil; my cup overflows. Psalm 23:5	**PSALM 23** 1/45/2 Forever Surely goodness and love will follow me all the days of my life, and I will dwell in the house of the LORD forever. . Psalm 23:6

Crook

In the pull-out chart a shepherd's crook is suggested as the symbol by which this theme is remembered.

Shepherd and sheep

The memory aid is "shepherd and sheep."

When you begin choosing your own symbols and memory aids for the themes you select for learning in year 2, there is nothing wrong with choosing obvious and straightforward ideas such as "shepherd and sheep." However, memory training experts suggest that we are more likely to remember things if we use ideas which are:

• moving
• funny – the more humorous the better
• memorable

Topics for Psalm 23

The topics for each verse for Psalm 23 are as follows:

Psalm 23:1	Shepherd
Psalm 23:2	Pasture
Psalm 23:3	Restores
Psalm 23:4	Comfort
Psalm 23:5	Anointed
Psalm 23:6	Forever

Remembering the topics

With such well-known verses and with consecutive verses, you may feel that you do not need any further help in remembering the topics.

But if you do, work out how you are going to remember the words "Shepherd, Pasture, Restores, Comfort, Anointed," and "Forever" in a memorable way. One way to remember key words is to picture them in an unusual setting – on the top of the Empire State Building, for example.

Weeks 46–52: 1 Corinthians 13

1 CORINTHIANS 12 1/46/1	**1 CORINTHIANS 13** 1/46/2	**1 CORINTHIANS 13** 1/47/1
Excellent way	Tongues	Prophecy
But eagerly desire the greater gifts. And now I will show you the most excellent way. 1 Corinthians 12:31	If I speak in the tongues of men and of angels, but have not love, I am only a resounding gong or a clanging cymbal. 1 Corinthians 13:1	If I have the gift of prophecy and can fathom all mysteries and all knowledge, and if I have a faith that can move mountains, but have not love, I am nothing. 1 Corinthians 13:2

1 CORINTHIANS 13 1/47/2	**1 CORINTHIANS 13** 1/48/1	**1 CORINTHIANS 13** 1/48/2
Giving	Patient	Not rude
If I give all I possess to the poor and surrender my body to the flames, but have not love, I gain nothing. 1 Corinthians 13:3	Love is patient, love is kind. It does not envy, it does not boast, it is not proud. 1 Corinthians 13:4	It is not rude, it is not self-seeking, it is not easily angered, it keeps no record of wrongs. 1 Corinthians 13:5

1 CORINTHIANS 13 1/49/1	**1 CORINTHIANS 13** 1/49/2	**1 CORINTHIANS 13** 1/50/1
Rejoices in truth	Trusts	Never fails
Love does not delight in evil but rejoices with the truth. 1 Corinthians 13:6	It always protects, always trusts, always hopes, always perseveres. 1 Corinthians 13:7	Love never fails. But where there are prophecies, they will cease; where there are tongues, they will be stilled; where there is knowledge, it will pass away. 1 Corinthians 13:8

1 CORINTHIANS 13 1/50/2 Partial For we know in part and we prophesy in part, 1 Corinthians 13:9	**1 CORINTHIANS 13** 1/51/1 Perfection but when perfection comes, the imperfect disappears. 1 Corinthians 13:10	**1 CORINTHIANS 13** 1/51/2 Face to face When I was a child, I talked like a child, I thought like a child, I reasoned like a child. When I became a man, I put childish ways behind me. 1 Corinthians 13:11

1 CORINTHIANS 13 1/52/1 Childish ways Now we see but a poor reflection as in a mirror; then we shall see face to face. Now I know in part; then I shall know fully, even as I am fully known. 1 Corinthians 13:12	**1 CORINTHIANS 13** 1/52/2 The greatest And now these three remain: faith, hope and love. But the greatest of these is love. 1 Corinthians 13:13

Heart symbol
In the pull-out chart you will see that a heart symbol has been used to remember 1 Corinthians 13. The idea comes from an old Beatles song which says "All you need is love; yeah, yeah, yeah."

Topics
The topics for remembering the theme of 1 Corinthians are:

1 Corinthians

12:31	Excellent way	13:7	Trusts
13:1	Tongues	13:8	Never fails
13:2	Prophecy	13:9	Partial
13:3	Giving	13:10	Perfection
13:4	Patient	13:11	Face to face
13:5	Not rude	13:12	Childish ways
13:6	Rejoices in truth	13:13	The greatest

You may want to devise a catchy way to remember the order of these fourteen verses.

How to make your plan for next year

1. Make your own collection

As you read through the Bible this year, jot down any Bible verses that strike you as being ideal verses to remember. Keep a piece of paper in your Bible for this purpose. Then arrange them into themes. You just need one hundred to be all set for next year.

2. Memorize chapters

If you want to remember sections of the Bible, then the following chapters and parts of chapters would be suitable ones.

- *Isaiah 52:13–53:12*
- *John 15:1–27*
- *Romans 8:1–39*
- *Philippians 2:1–18*

These four passages make up one hundred verses.

3. Review plan

Work out your own review plan. Base it on the review plan for the year on pages 16-17, "How do I review verses?"

4. Memory helps

Provide memory helps for each theme as you go along. Try to work out an overall plan so your themes fit into the fifty-two weeks of the year.

Sharing your Faith made easy

It's no good pretending that all Christians are keen on personally spreading the Christian message. Talking on a one-to-one basis about our own personal faith in Jesus is just not on the agenda for most of us.

Much of what goes under the label of "witnessing" is nothing short of a well-meaning Christian opening his or her mouth and putting his or her foot in it!

If we are going to spread the gospel, we need to know how to get started. And we need to know what to say to different types of people: atheists, agnostics and those who belong to other faiths.

The English Bible teacher, John Stott, once told his congregation, "I want you not to be afraid to speak for Jesus Christ."

Sharing your faith made easy was written to help explore how to speak for Jesus Christ.

Contents

By way of introduction

1. Jesus' first *words to his disciples*
For many Christians the whole idea of
sharing one's faith is:

"Fishers of men"

• a giant turn off
• a total embarrassment
• a puzzle – "How can I do it?"

When Jesus called his first disciples to follow him he gave them
this promise:

"I will make you fishers of men [and women]." *Matthew 4:19*

Conclusion No 1: Jesus says he will help us to share him with others.

2. Jesus' last *words to his disciples*
For many other Christians sharing one's
faith is treated as:

"Make disciples"

• an optional extra – "I may, if I feel like it."
• a non-starter – "If Jesus wants to convert the world,
  he could do it without my help."

When Jesus left his eleven faithful followers he gave them this
command:

"Go and make disciples of all nations." *Matthew 28:19.*

Conclusion No 2: Jesus commands us to share our faith.

---

3. Why should we share our faith?

**We *don't* share our faith
because**

• We feel we're not up to it
• We are good/bad at it

**We *do* share Jesus with others
because**

• Jesus promised us his help.
• Jesus told us to do it.

This book will give you some handy hints on how to begin
sharing your faith.

Be reasonable

Advice from an elderly fisherman
"... Always be prepared to give an answer to everyone who asks you to give the reason for the hope that you have. But do this with gentleness and respect."
1 Peter 3:15

Where to witness	Look up and read
1. Throughout the world	Mark 16:15-16
2. To strangers	John 12:20-22
3. In your home	Mark 5:19
4. In unexpected places	Acts 8:26-40
5. Among your friends	John 1:45-49

6

1 Peter 3:15

1. "Always ..."

2. "... be prepared"

3. "... to give an answer ..."

4. "... to everyone ..."

5. "... give the reason ..."

6. "... for the hope you have."

7. "... do this with gentleness and respect."

HOW TO SHARE YOUR FAITH
Hot tip No 1:
Don't argue. Do not let your discussion turn into a full scale war of words. Keep cool. Try not to lose your temper! Remember: it's possible to win the argument and lose the battle.

The very practical Peter

1. *Always* means always or at all times. There is no day or time of day when we are off duty as Christians.

2. *Be prepared* means make preparations to help you to share your faith. Reading through a book like this is one way to do this. Become fully familiar with the Bible.

3. *To give an answer* means that there are answers to give. You may not know all the answers now. You may never know *all* the answers. But this does not stop you from finding out some answers when you get stuck. Make use of more experienced Christians. See if one of them can help you.

4. *Everyone* means everyone (no omissions, no exceptions). You can't be too choosy who you witness to. God may give you many different kinds of people that you should witness to.

5. *Give the reason* means that the Christian faith is not anti-reason. Oh, yes, it is *faith*, but we have all been given minds by God. God commands us to love him with our *minds*. It brings no credit to Jesus if we give the impression that Christianity is irrational. If that was the case it would mean that a human mind is superior to God's mind.

6. *For the hope you have* means that we must share the hope and confidence that we have in Jesus as our Savior.

7. *Do this with gentleness and respect* means that we treat people with a kindly, understanding spirit. We don't turn people off by our attitude or demeanor.

See also: *Pray, pray, pray,* pages 38-39; *Don't ever forget the Holy Spirit,* pages 56-57.

Focus on Jesus

"The church has nothing to do but to save souls; therefore spend and be spent in this work."
John Wesley

Jesus in the Acts of the Apostles
Jesus is the central theme throughout the Acts of the Apostles and should be our central focus.
- Peter said to the cripple who begged for money outside the temple: "Silver and gold I do not have, but what I have I give you. In the name of *Jesus Christ* of Nazareth walk." *Acts 3:6*
- To the astonished crowd who saw Peter heal this cripple, Peter said, "The God of our fathers ... has glorified his servant *Jesus*." *Acts 3:13*

The name of Jesus in the Acts of the Apostles
- In the 28 chapters of the Acts of the Apostles, *Jesus* is mentioned in over 70 verses.
- A great Bible study is to read one chapter of the Acts of the Apostles each day.
- Check out each time *Jesus* is the focus of attention for the first Christians.
- List every verse in which *Jesus* appears, with a note on the theme of the verse.
- The only chapters in which the name of *Jesus* is not seen are 12, 14, 23, 27.

Acts chapter 1	What is said about Jesus?
Verse 1	Jesus was the main theme of the gospel of Luke.
Verse 11	Jesus' ascension. Jesus will come again.
Verse 14	The virgin Mary was known as "the mother of Jesus."
Verse 16	Judas acted as a guide to those who arrested Jesus.
Verse 21	One of the qualifications for the new apostle was that he had to have known Jesus while he was on this earth.
Verse 22	Jesus' death and his resurrection.

Jesus in the Acts, even when not mentioned by name

Continuing in the Acts of the Apostles, read through one chapter at a time, and list the verses in which Jesus is referred to, but *not* mentioned by name.

The verses in chapter 1, where the name of Jesus is not mentioned, but which still have a direct reference to him are: 2, 3, 4, 5, 6, 7, 8, 9, 10, 12, 23, 24, 25.

Acts chapter 1	Where Jesus is referred to but not mentioned by name
Verse 2	Jesus' ascension
Verse 3	Jesus' death and resurrection
Verse 4	Jesus promises the coming of the Holy Spirit
Verse 5	Jesus promises that his disciples will be baptized by the Holy Spirit
Verses 6-7	Jesus answers a question from the disciples
Verse 8	Jesus tells his disciples to be his witnesses
Verses 9-10	Jesus' ascension
Verse 12	The promise that Jesus will come again
Verse 25	The apostolic ministry by Jesus' special disciples

Remember what Jesus said about himself

"I am the way and the truth and the life. No one comes to the Father except through me." *John 14:6.*

What about other religions?

It may sound almost arrogant to imply that Jesus is the only way – that there is something wrong with all other religions. But here we are dealing with a *truth* question.

This is one Bible verse that makes uncomfortable reading if one is a Jew, a Buddhist, a Hindu or a Muslim.

"Salvation is found in no one else, for there is no other name under heaven given to men by which we must be saved." Acts 4:12.

Jesus is *the* way to God. There may be many paths which lead to Christ, but Jesus is the *only* way to God.

Listen before you leap

Different approaches

Have you ever considered how many different ways Jesus spoke to people when they came to him? His approach was never the same.

Because he listened to them, he knew their specific spiritual need. What he said always met that immediate need.

Listen, listen, listen

To find out where people are spiritually, we need to pray for the Holy Spirit to help us, and to listen to what people say. Listen to their words. Observe their body language. Listen before you leap in with the gospel. Then what you say will meet their individual spiritual need.

What Jesus said to whom

In Matthew's gospel:

The person/the people	Jesus' instruction	
1. To the man with leprosy	"Be clean."	*Matthew 8:3*
2. To the believing centurion	"It will be done as you believed it would"	*Matthew 8:13*
3. To the Canaanite woman	"Your request is granted."	*Matthew 15:28*
4. To the rich young man	"Sell your possessions and give to the poor."	*Matthew 19:21*

In John's gospel:

The person/the people	Jesus' instruction	
1. To Philip	"Follow me."	*John 1:43*
2. To Nicodemus	"You must be born again."	*John 3:7*
3. To the Samaritan woman who wanted water	"I give ... a spring of water welling up to eternal life."	*John 4:14*
4. To the man who had not walked for thirty-eight years	"Get up! ... and walk."	*John 5:8*
5. To the man born blind	"I am the light of the world."	*John 9:5*
6. To Jews asking, "Are you the Christ?"	"I give eternal life."	*John 10:28*
7. To Martha in her bereavement	"I am the resurrection and the life"	*John 11:25*

What is the best book on **how can I share Jesus?**
The best book to learn more about witnessing for Jesus is the New Testament. Go through Mark's and Luke's Gospel and make similar tables to the one above.
• Note the variety of people Jesus spoke to.
• Note how what Jesus said fit exactly what that person needed to hear.

The ABCD of sharing your faith

"He who wins souls is wise." *Proverbs 11:30*
So, how does one go about "winning souls": that is, introducing people to Jesus?

There are countless ways. Here is one very simple way. If you find it helpful, you can make use of it. If you don't find it helpful, you can try some other way. It's not meant to be a slick technique. It is simply a straightforward way of helping someone who wants to know how to make the Lord Jesus Christ to become their friend and Savior.

ABCD
This is just a useful way for you to remember four things, as you attempt to lead a person to Jesus. You go through four things, from A to D.

A stands for *Admit*
B stands for *Believe*
C stands for *Come to Jesus*
D stands for *Details*

The next eight pages go through each of these.

What do I actually say?
Over the next eight pages there are sections to suggest what you actually say, as you go through the ABCD of the plan of salvation. Now you don't have to use these words; you can say the same thing using your own words.

- The *What do I actually say?* sections are put there to make it crystal clear what point you are trying to cover at each stage.
- In the same way the *What do I actually pray?* section is only a guide. You can use totally different words and still be praying for the same thing.

- Also, in the *What do I actually write?* section, the letter is only a guide and you can make up your own to cover the same things. The *What do I actually ...?* sections are intended to be examples for people who want help, step-by-step.

It's a friendship with a friend

- Being a Christian is being a friend with Jesus.
- Becoming a Christian is starting this friendship.

  Don't be confused by the many different ways in which this friendship is described in the Bible and by Christians today. Sometimes you read about or hear the following phrases – don't worry, they all mean the same thing.

"Coming to Christ"

"Turning to Jesus"

"Putting one's faith in Jesus"

"Accepting Christ"

"Becoming a Christian"

"Inviting Jesus into my life"

"Being converted"

"Being born again"

"Being born from above"

"Being born by the Spirit"

"I was forgiven by Jesus"

"I came to know Jesus as my friend"

"Committing yourself to Jesus"

"I started to follow Christ"

"You are a new person in Jesus"

Try not to confuse the person you are sharing your faith with. The best thing to do is to follow one way of speaking about "becoming a Christian." Try to stick to that one way.

One of the most helpful ways to do this is to talk about Jesus being a friend.

A is for Admit

The spiritual condition of those who do not know Jesus	
Their spiritual state	**Look up and read**
1. They are in a state of death	*Romans 6:23*
2. They are perishing	*1 Corinthians 1:18*
3. They have no hope	*Ephesians 2:12*
4. They are condemned by God	*John 3:18*
5. They are spiritually dead	*Ephesians 2:1*
6. They are under God's wrath	*John 3:36*
7. They have neither God nor Jesus	*Ephesians 2:12*

It's not necessary that the person you are trying to introduce to Jesus knows all this! You're just trying to help them to get started. But it is helpful for you to realize what the Bible teaches about everyone being a sinner in God's eyes.

What do I actually say?
"It's so wonderful that you want to ask Jesus to be your Friend.

The Bible explains that we need to start by admitting something. We need to acknowledge that we are sinful in God's sight.

Here's a helpful verse in the Bible about this. 'All have sinned and fall short of the glory of God.' *Romans 3:23*

Everyone in the world has sinned.

God is perfect and we are far from being perfect. This is what the Bible calls sin.

To sin: is to violate God's law, to miss the mark of perfection or to step outside the boundary of right into wrong.

The first thing you have to do in order to have Jesus as your friend is to admit that you are a sinner."

14

Don't *worry* if ...
- You get tongue-tied.
- You find that you are embarrassed. Do your best to focus on the person you are trying to help and to forget about yourself.
- You drop your Bible, forget a Bible verse or lose your way. Remember A, B, C, D and then cover each point as best as you can.

Do *worry* if ...
- You think this is too easy for words and it is something you will just sail through.
- You don't pray before you start and after you have finished.
- You are not humbled that God should use you to introduce someone to Jesus
- You ever lose the wonder of this.

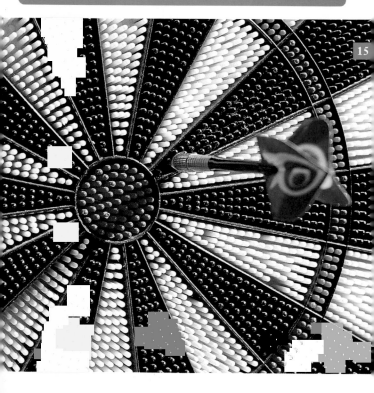

B is for Believe

What do I actually say?

"To have Jesus as your Friend, the Bible says that you need to believe that he can help you.

Since we are all sinners in God's sight, Jesus came into our world to help us.

Jesus came to deal with our sin problem. This verse offers help to understand this. It tells us why Jesus died on the cross. 'He himself [that is, Jesus] bore our sins in his own body on the tree [that is, the cross].' *1 Peter 2:24*

The apostle Peter says that Jesus took our sins on himself when he died on the cross. Let me illustrate this:

1. Here I am *(put out your left hand)*
2. Because, like everyone, I am a sinner, it's as if I'm weighed down and burdened by sin *(put a large object such as a book, wallet, car keys on a clean handkerchief into the palm of your left hand. This object is to represent sin).*
3. When Jesus died on the cross for us, he took our sin on himself. *(Turn your left hand over into the palm of your right hand so that the object used is now in your right hand. Hold out your empty left hand. The object is now gone. Then hold out your right hand with the object sitting in your palm.)*

4. Now *(move your left hand up and down two or three times)* our sin (and the weight of our sin) has been taken away from us.
5. This verse is saying that it's easy to see where our sin is. It's been placed on Jesus

(move your right hand – with the object in the palm of your hand – up and down two or three times.)

The second thing you have to do for Jesus to be your friend is to believe that Jesus died for you."

Some more handy hints

• You don't have to repeat the Bible references to the person you are speaking to.
• Memorize the Bible verses you use.
• Write down the verses on the inside back cover of your Bible. Then you won't worry in case you forget them (if you have memorized them) or that you may remember them incorrectly. Here's how to write them down.

A stands for	Admit that I am a sinner	Romans 3:23	Page number ... *(of your Bible)*
B stands for	Believe that Jesus died for me	1 Peter 2:24	Page number ...
C stands for	Come to Jesus	Revelation 3:20	Page number ...

17

See also: *The Bridge*, pages 40-41

C is for Come to Jesus

What do I actually say?

"Once you are ready to admit that you are a sinner … once you believe that Jesus took your sin on him when he died for you … it is time for action. The third thing necessary to have Jesus as your friend – is to do something.

The Bible explains how we start our friendship with Jesus in this verse. 'Here I am! I stand at the door and knock. If anyone hears my voice and opens the door, I will come in and eat with him, and he with me.' *Revelation 3:20*

This verse pictures Jesus standing outside a door. The idea is that he is trying to get into a house and he is knocking at the door.

The door represents our lives. Jesus knocks on the door of our lives and he wants us to open the door and say, 'Come in. Please come in Lord Jesus.'

Until now Jesus has been, as it were, outside your life. Having Jesus as your friend means asking him to step inside (into) your life.

So the third thing you have to do in order to have Jesus as your friend is to come to Jesus and invite him into your life."

A prayer asking Jesus into a person's life

"Would you like to invite Jesus into your life now and have him as your friend? *(If the answer is 'yes,' or a nod of the head, continue.)*

Would you like me to lead you in a personal prayer that you make your own – asking Jesus into your life? *(If the answer is 'yes,' or a nod of the head, continue.)*"

What do I actually pray?

"Here is a prayer you can pray line by line after me. You can pray it audibly or silently. 'Lord Jesus Christ *(pause for a second or two at the end of each line to allow time for the person you are helping to pray the prayer)*, I know that I have sinned and am sorry for my sins. *(Pause)*

Thank you for dying on the cross to take away my sin. *(Pause)*
I want you to be my special friend. *(Pause)*
Please come into my life now. *(Pause)*
I want you as my Savior and friend for ever. *(Pause)*
Amen. *(Pause)*"

19

A prayer for you to pray

If the person has prayed the above prayer, pray a prayer along the following lines. This is a prayer you are praying and is not like the above prayer which is a prayer for the other person to pray.

"Lord Jesus Christ thank you for coming into ____'s *(say the person's name here, and in the following blanks)* life.

Please help ____ to become a closer and closer friend with you throughout his/her life.

Please help ____ to find help from other Christians.

Please help ____ to serve you all his/her life, with the help of the Holy Spirit. Amen."

D is for details

1. Because baptism is the initial reaction to accepting Christ in the New Testament – be certain the person gives attention to this need to be baptized

Throughout the New Testament a person's initial reaction to accepting Jesus as their Savior was to submit to baptism. Baptism depicts two things. First, it depicts as an object lesson the death, the burial and the resurrection of Jesus. Secondly, it portrays for the Christian the death to sin, the burial of the old life and the resurrection to a new life. For further study on this topic, see *Matthew 3:13-17; Acts 2:37-39; 8:26-40; 16:25-34; and Romans 6:3-7.*

2. Make sure the person is linked up to a helpful Christian fellowship

Determine whether the person already goes to a church where he/she will find spiritual help. If not, ask if you can take his/her name and address/phone number. You need to get the person's permission for you to aid them in finding a church that will help provide spiritual growth. Then provide the individual with the details.

3. Encourage the person to read the Bible every day

It is very important for the person to read the Bible for him/herself and to pray each day. Make certain that the person has a Bible, some Bible helps or tools and then provide some instructions.

If you don't have any Bible helps to pass on say, "Try reading one chapter from Mark's Gospel each day. And then move on and do the same with Matthew, Luke and John."

4. Write a letter

If the individual lives far away, a personal letter from you is likely to be appreciated.

Points to cover

1. "How wonderful that you have asked Jesus to be your Friend." Without preaching a sermon you need to cover the following points, especially if the person is not linked up to a Christian fellowship.

2. "The friendship you have just started is the beginning of a new life with Jesus.

There are a number of things helpful in a friendship with Jesus:

a. Keep on deepening your friendship with Jesus. Pray to him daily plus make Bible reading a part of each day. These activities will help to make Jesus more real.

b. Tell other people about Jesus, even though this can be difficult at times. How you live is as important in witnessing as what you say.

c. Join with other Christians in worship and in informal times of praising God. It is also helpful to get involved in a weekly Bible study."

3. If you have details about a helpful church, provide them.

4. Close by saying that you will be praying for him/her. If you intend to pray for him/her every day, you should tell them so.

More follow-up

Paul's aim

Paul never said that it was his aim to win as many people as possible for Jesus. Paul did say, "We proclaim [Jesus] ... so that we may present everyone perfect in Christ." *Colossians 1:28*.

It's hard to overemphasize the importance of follow-up.

Follow-up means making sure that a new Christian has the means to survive and grow.

Wesley and Whitefield

John Wesley and George Whitefield were both greatly used by God as they preached in America and through the length and breadth of England.

At the end of his life Whitefield admitted that he wished he had been like Wesley in his follow-up methods. Wesley tried to make sure that all the people who became Christians through his preaching joined in a local, weekly meeting with other Christians, so they could pray, study the Bible together, and offer one another guidance and encouragement.

Whitefield wrote in his Journal
"My brother Wesley acted more wisely than I. The souls that were awakened under his ministry he joined together in classes, and so preserved the fruit of his labors. I failed to do this, and as a result my people are a rope of sand."

Wesley wrote in his Journal
"I determined by the grace of God not to strike one blow in any place where I cannot follow the blow."

Follow up is part of leading someone to Jesus

Don't think that your work is over once you've helped someone to accept Christ as Savior. Your work may have only just started.

Your responsibility is to make sure that they have the means to be linked up to a Christian fellowship.

When people become Christians they are said to be spiritual babies. They are like "newborn babies" according to Peter, see *1 Peter 2:2.*

Human babies take many years before they can stand on their own feet and fend for themselves. Follow up work may take many years.

What you can do

Your job is not to make them grow spiritually, only the Holy Spirit does that. Your job is to encourage and guide.

Sometimes all you will have to do is to pass along their name to another Christian or church leader who will take on this responsibility. Sometimes you will be able to do some or all of the following things:

1. Pray daily for the person.

2. Write a follow up letter.

3. Ensure that the person has information about a local helpful Christian group.

What are the marks of a good church? Look for a church where:
a. Jesus Christ is at the center of the worship and all activities
b. The Bible is preached and taken seriously

4. Provide helpful introductory Bible reading suggestions.

5. Pass along a booklet that explains how one becomes a Christian. It is especially important to choose one which explains about assurance (being sure that one is a Christian). If there is no confidence and security as a Christian, then, as Jesus said, "The evil one comes and snatches what was sown in his heart." *Matthew 13:19.* If you think that a person won't read such a booklet you may have to write a letter, simply explaining what assurance and security in Christ means. See pages 24-25.

Using the Bible

The Bible is your authority

Your own ultimate authority in matters about the Christian faith is the Bible. So when you share your faith, you should not continually say, "I think this, I think that." The person you are talking needs to know that your ideas are based on what the Bible says. So, instead of saying, "What I think about sin is ..."; you may say, "What the Bible teaches about sin is ..."

Some people like to ask the person they are trying to lead to Jesus to read out aloud the Bible verses they are referring to. This may help to make the point that your authority comes from the Bible. (However, this may be too much of an ordeal for some people who may not be too familiar with the Bible and it could turn out to be embarrassing for them.)

Remember: all Scripture is inspired by God

"All Scripture is God-breathed and is useful for teaching, rebuking, correcting and training in righteousness, so that the man of God may be thoroughly equipped for every good work." *2 Timothy 3:16*

Being sure that Jesus is your friend

Here's a draft paragraph about Christian assurance you could include in a follow up letter. You will see that it takes a Bible verse as the basis for what it says.

What do I actually write?

Many new Christians have doubts and wonder if Jesus really did become their friend. If that happens to you, you may like to know that this is quite normal! Here is a plan of action to counter such doubts.

1. Read the verse from Revelation chapter three, verse twenty, in your own Bible.
"Here I am! I stand at the door and knock. If anyone hears my voice and opens the door, I will come in and eat with him, and he with me."

2. Ask yourself: "Did I sincerely ask Jesus to come into my life?"

3. Note carefully the promise Jesus makes in this verse. What does he say if someone does open the door to him?

4. Jesus' promise is: "I will come in."
He does *not* say, "I may come in."
He does *not* say, "I will come in but will leave you if you sin."

5. Jesus has promised to enter the door of your life if you invite him in. As a result you can rest assured that he has come into your life and that he is your Friend. We need to remember that Jesus is the Son of God and we are putting our trust in him and his promises and not in ourselves and our doubts.

Another good passage on Christian assurance: 1 John 5:11-13

Verse 11: And this is the testimony: God has given us eternal life, and this life is in his Son.

Verse 12: He who has the Son has life; he who does not have the Son of God does not have life.

Verse 13: I write these things to you who believe in the name of the Son of God so that you may know that you have eternal life.

These verses teach:
  a. that God wants us to *know* that we have eternal life, that is life with Jesus for ever;
  b. that eternal life is God's gift to us;
  c. that we have eternal life as we have believed in Jesus.

The power of the written word

Have a Bible study

- Have a Bible study with an unconverted friend. Many people think only of having Bible studies with other Christians. But for a person who really wants to learn about Jesus Christ, there is no better way to help him/her than to have a Bible study together.
- Have a Bible study with a brand new Christian.

What should we study?

- For a non-Christian try John 3:1-16, and for a second Bible study, John 4:1-54.
- For a new Christian you could go through the theme of the way of salvation. Here are some headings with the relevant Bible verses to look up and discuss.

The way of salvation

A is for Admit: Admitting that we are sinners and need Jesus: *Romans 3:23; Romans 6:23; Isaiah 59:2*

B is for Belief: Believing in Jesus and his death for us: *Isaiah 53:5-6; 1 Peter 3:18; 1 Peter 2:24*

C is for Coming to Jesus: *Revelation 3:20; John 1:12; Acts 8:26-40*

Verses on Christian assurance: *1 John 5:11-13; John 6:37*

Letter of dedication

Some people have found it very reassuring to have a written record about the moment they asked Jesus to be their Friend. You could suggest the following as suitable wording for a new Christian to write out and keep.

> Lord Jesus,
> I admit that I am a sinner.
> I want to turn from my sin.
> I believe that you died for my sin.
> Please come into my life
> to be my Friend and Savior.
> Amen.
>
> Signature ....
>
> Date ....

The ministry of Christian literature

- Find some up-to-date booklets that explain how to begin living the Christian life.
- Other useful booklets for new Christians are:

a. Daily Devotionals and Read through the Bible guides. These are available for different age groups and different levels of Christian understanding.

b. Evangelistic tracts. These often contain true conversion stories.

One short visit to a Christian Bookstore would help you stock up with many of these witnessing/sharing resources.

Some Christians set aside money each month to buy Christian books and booklets for other people.

See also: *Using the Internet*, page 64

A link in the chain

Paul's conversion

We often think that the most famous conversion of all time came out of the blue and that Jesus spoke directly to Paul without any human being involved.

A flash of light from heaven

Read through Paul's conversion in **Acts 9:1-20** and see how wonderfully Paul met with the risen Lord Jesus.

v.1-2 Some people are converted when they least expect it.

v.3-4 Nobody is beyond being converted by God. Many of the worst persecutors of Christians have themselves become converted.

v.5 It became clear to Saul that he was having an encounter with Jesus.

v.6 Saul had to be told. He did not himself know what to do.

v.7 Other people are often mystified by the Christian conversion process.

v.10 Ananias was alert to God. Have you ever thought how important Ananias was in Paul's conversion?

v.11 Humanly speaking, Paul would have been nowhere without Ananias.

v.12 When God wants you to speak to someone, he will prepare the person.

v.13-15 Sometimes we have to expect the unexpected. Even Ananias got some things wrong but because he was obedient God overruled.

v.16 Living the Christian life involves difficulties. It's not all easy sailing.

v.17 All true conversions center on Jesus and the Holy Spirit.

v.18 Baptism was a sign and culmination of conversion.

v.19 Fellowship with other Christians is vital for new Christians.

v.20 Few new Christians openly witness about Jesus more quickly than Paul did!

Giving your testimony

When a Christian tells a group of people how he/she became a Christian it is sometimes called giving one's testimony.

The idea is that the Christian should be sharing about God's grace and about the way he/she came to commit his/her life to

Jesus. If you are ever asked to do this, there are two pitfalls to be aware of:
• Don't imply that it was more spectacular than it really was;
• And point to Jesus and not to yourself.

John the Baptist got it exactly right when he said, speaking of Jesus, "He must become greater; I must become less." *John 3:30*

Paul never tired of giving his testimony. Luke records it three times. *See Acts 9:1-19; Acts 22:4-16; 26:9-18*

A link in the chain

You could say that there were a number of hidden factors behind Paul's conversion.

We do not know just how much of an impression Stephen's martyrdom had on Paul.

Clearly Luke thought it was significant as he says that the people who stoned Stephen to death, "laid their clothes at the feet of a young man named Saul." *Acts 7:58*

Luke concludes Stephen's martyrdom by saying, "And Saul was there, giving approval to his death." *Acts 8:1*

When you seek to share your faith remember that you are one link in a chain.

• You may be the first link, setting someone thinking about God in general.	• You may be a middle link, helping someone to see clearly who Jesus is.	• You may be the last link, showing someone how they can ask Jesus into their lives.

Planting and watering

Paul angrily scolded the Christians at Corinth for splitting themselves into divisive groups and then following particular Christian leaders.

Paul's answer to all this was to say, "I planted the seed, Apollos watered it, but God made it grow." *1 Corinthians 3:6*

So it does not matter which link in the chain you are. The important thing is for us to do our part faithfully and to remember that God is the one who carries out his work in people's lives. "God makes his seed grow."

I've never done this before

"Even if I were utterly selfish and had no care for anything but my own happiness I would choose, if I might, under God, to be a soul-winner; for never did I know perfect overflowing, unutterable happiness of the purest and most ennobling order till I first heard of one who had sought and found the Savior through my means.

"No young mother ever so rejoiced over her first born child, no warrior was so exultant over a hard won victory." *C.H. Spurgeon*

Know-how or courage?

For most people lack of courage, rather than lack of know-how, stops them from sharing their faith.

There are ways to build up your courage.

Building block one – overcoming the fear of rejection

Jesus said that we should expect to be persecuted. "They persecuted me, they will persecute you." *John 15:20.*

Now, nobody likes to be rejected or laughed at, or thought to be a religious fanatic. Someone has said that it is easier to face guns than to face grins.

a. Pray and ask others to pray for you

We have to ask God for courage to overcome our fear of being rejected or we'll never start. Paul was only too aware of his own fears in sharing the gospel. He asked other Christians to pray for him about such matters. We should do exactly the same. Paul wrote, "Pray also for me, that whenever I open my mouth, words may be given me so that I will fearlessly make known the mystery of the gospel." *Ephesians 6:19.*

b. Be a fool for Jesus

Be prepared to be a fool for Jesus, especially when you are made fun of. Paul wrote, "We are fools for Christ." *1 Corinthians 4:10.*

c. Please God not people

Sort out in your mind who you are trying to please. Are you trying to keep up appearances before people, or are you trying to serve God? Peter was hauled before the top Jewish Council, the Sanhedrin, accused (as if it was a crime) of peaching about Jesus. Peter's bold reply was: "We must obey God rather than men!" *Acts 5:29.*

Building block two – Do something you *can* manage

If you find the idea of witnessing to total strangers too much to cope with, do something that you can manage.

You may find it easier to write to, or e-mail somebody about Jesus rather than talking to them face to face or phoning them.

Possibly it may be easier to give an evangelistic booklet than explain the way of salvation yourself. If this is so, carry around with you some tracts, so you can give them away at the appropriate time. Some people even enclose tracts when paying their bills! You may be able to lend a Christian video or Christian book to a friend.

Develop a positive rather than a negative attitude. Don't say, "I can't preach in public. I can't witness to strangers. I don't think I'll do anything!" Do what you can do. Don't worry about what you can't do.

HOW TO SHARE YOUR FAITH
Hot tip No 2:

Start your own note book. Every time you learn something that is going to help you share your faith, write it down in your notebook. As a reminder of the lesson you learned, put a date beside it. This will help you reflect back on what you learned on that day.

Go for variety

Paul as a model soul-winner

Why did Paul witness to Jesus?	Look up and read	More verses to look up and read
1. Because he was commanded to:	*Romans 10:9-10*	*Matthew 10:32-33; Psalm 107:2*
2. Because he was not ashamed to:	*Romans 1:16*	
3. Because of what Jesus had done for him:	*Romans 5:1-2*	*Psalm 40:1-3*

All things to all people

Paul was often misunderstood – even by fellow Christians!

He cared more about helping people spiritually than about what other Christians might say.

He explained this when the wrote to the Christians at Corinth: "I have become all things to all men so that by all possible means I might save some." *1 Corinthians 9:22*

Paul's example	What does that mean for you?
"I have become all things ...	Certainly this would include showing a genuine interest in what other people are interested in – obviously, excluding things that are clearly evil!
... to all men ...	All men means all people – men and women. Paul knew how to appeal to top Jewish leaders, as well as to those who had no interest, whatsoever, in Christianity. This means that we should be happy to share our faith with all kinds of different people, without thinking about their background, age, class, race, profession or social standing.
... so that by all possible means ...	Paul used every available God-given means to spread the gospel. Today Christians have access to various forms of media that can be used for sharing their faith – the radio, TV, videos, the Internet, attractive Christians books, CD's and cassettes, and even computer software. (How about watching a Christian video with a friend who may not be ready to go to church with you?)
... I might save some."	Paul never lost sight of his goal – to be a means of introducing people to Jesus, the Savior.

HOW TO
SHARE YOUR FAITH
Hot tip No 3:
Conversion has been defined as: "Committing all I know of me to all I know of Christ." As you share your faith, point the person you are talking to, to Jesus.

What does "born again" mean?

Nicodemus goes to Jesus

The phrase comes from the conversation Nicodemus had with Jesus. *See John 3:1-16.*

Jesus said to him, "You must be born again." *John 3:7.*

It is one way of describing how one becomes a Christian. Books of theology sometimes call this the doctrine of regeneration. ("To bring new life and energy to that which is dead.")

What this new birth is **not**

• **The new birth is not being highly religious.**
If anyone could have reached heaven by living a religious life and doing good deeds it was Nicodemus. According to John 3:1 he was a Pharisee.

• **The new birth is not doing lots of good deeds.**
"For it is by grace you have been saved, through faith – and this not from yourselves, it is the gift of God – not by works, so that no one can boast." *Ephesians 2:8-9. See also Matthew 7:21-23*

Portrait of Nicodemus the Pharisee

• He fasted twice a week.
• He gave away 10% of his income.
• Every day he prayed for two hours in the synagogue.
• He had learned the first five books of the Bible – word for word.

But it was to this important Pharisee that Jesus said, "You must be born again." And Jesus told him this three times – in case he did not get the message the first time, which he did not!
See John 3:3, 5, 7

Some Bible definitions of new birth

- **A divine birth**
  "No one who is born of God will continue to sin, because God's seed remains in him; he cannot go on sinning, because he has been born of God." *1 John 3:9*
- **A new creation**
  "Therefore, if anyone is in Christ, he is a new creation; the old has gone, the new has come!" *2 Corinthians 5:17*
- **A spiritual awakening**
  "He saved us, not because of righteous things we had done, but because of his mercy. He saved us through the washing of rebirth and renewal by the Holy Spirit." *Titus 3:5*

The need, the way, and the result of a new birth

The need for a new birth

1. It is universal. Everyone needs it. *Jeremiah 17:9-10; Titus 3:3; Romans 3:23*
2. We cannot change ourselves. *Jeremiah 13:23; Ephesians 2:8-9*
3. Jesus said we must be born again. *John 3:3, 5, 7*
4. The new birth is essential because of God's holiness. *Hebrews 12:14*

The way to a new birth

1. By hearing and believing the gospel. *James 1:18; Romans 10:17*
2. It is God's work carried out by the Holy Spirit. *Titus 3:5; John 16:7-9*
3. By a personal decision to believe who Jesus is and trust him to do what he has promised. *Acts 16:31-33; John 1:12; Titus 3:5*

The result of a new birth

1. Becoming a child of God. *John 1:12-13*
2. The forgiveness of sin. *Acts 2:38-39*
3. The living presence of the Holy Spirit. *1 Corinthians 3:16-17*
4. Living a righteous life. *Titus 2:14; 1 John 2:29*
5. A love for fellow Christians. *1 John 3:14*

Dealing with diversions and smoke screens

Jesus speaks with the woman from Samaria

There is perhaps no better example in the New Testament of how to do personal evangelism, than the story of Jesus speaking with the woman from Samaria.

Work your way through John 4:1-42 and see how many lessons you can learn from seeing Jesus the master winner of souls at work.

A summary of John 4:1-42

Verses	What Jesus did
1-7	Jesus made contact
8-15	Jesus aroused her spiritual interest
16-18	Jesus did not ignore her sin
19-24	Jesus dealt with her diversionary tactic
25-26	Jesus challenged her to commit herself to him

How Jesus dealt with a red herring

"Sir," the woman said, "I can see that you are a prophet. Our fathers worshiped on this mountain, but you Jews claim that the place where we must worship is in Jerusalem."

Jesus declared, "Believe me, woman, a time is coming when you will worship the Father neither on this mountain nor in Jerusalem. You Samaritans worship what you do not know; we worship what we do know, for salvation is from the Jews. Yet a time is coming and has now come when the true worshipers will worship the Father in spirit and truth, for they are the kind of worshipers the Father seeks. God is spirit, and his worshipers must worship in spirit and in truth."
Verses 19-24

What the woman tried to do

Jesus' probing question was getting too close for comfort. She tried to steer the conversation away from herself, her sinful life and her spiritual need of God. She was looking for a less personal question.

How Jesus refused to be diverted

Jesus did answer her question, but immediately redirected the conversation back into a spiritual direction. He said, "God is spirit, and his worshipers must worship in spirit and truth."

Dealing with diversions

- Distinguish between a diversion and a genuine question.
- Remember: you don't have to answer a person's diversionary tactic the moment it is raised. You could say, "That's a very interesting question. Would you mind if we left it on one side for the time being?" And then return to the spiritual issue you are talking about.
- When God is convicting a person they usually try every way possible to escape. So don't be surprised by smoke screens, but don't let them divert you from the main purpose of your conversation.

Frequently raised diversions and smoke screens

What kind of answer could you give to these questions and difficulties if they were raised as you were trying to lead a person to Jesus? (Don't be a know-it-all.) Admit to doubts and difficulties when you have them.

1. What about other religions?
2. Did God create the world in seven days?
3. I have a different idea about God than you have.
4. I don't believe in the existence of God.
5. I don't believe that the Bible is the word of God.
6. How can you place such trust in the Bible? Isn't it full of contradictions?
7. I don't believe that Jesus was the Son of God.
8. What about all the suffering in the world?

12 lessons on soul winning from John 4

The lesson	Other verses
1. Make the most of any opportunity. *v.7*	*Colossians 4:5*
2. Establish contact through asking a question. *v.7*	*Luke 18:40*
3. Don't be aggressive. Be ready to admit your own need. *v.7*	*James 3:17-18*
4. Don't be put off by a lack of spiritual understanding. *v.10*	*1 Corinthians 2:14*
5. Talk about God and his gift of salvation. *v.10*	*Romans 6:23*
6. Draw spiritual truths from everyday things. *vv.10-12*	*Matthew 6:26-28*
7. Keep the conversation on spiritual matters. *v.13*	*John 3:3*
8. Show how appealing and satisfying Jesus is. *vv.13-14*	*Psalm 107:9; Acts 10:38*
9. Confront the sinner with the fact that he/she is a sinner. *v.16*	*Romans 3:23*
10. Watch out for diversions and smoke screens. *vv.19-21*	*Mark 9:33-37*
11. Do not be vague and fuzzy. *v.25*	*John 11:25*
12. God reveals himself through Jesus and his word. *v.26*	*Matthew 16:16-17*

Pray, pray, pray

The priority of prayer
Prayer is an important element in sharing your faith.

How to pray for yourself
- Pray that you may be close to Jesus.
- Pray that you will be used by Jesus.
- Pray when you are at the point of sharing your faith. Pray as you are about to speak. Pray as you knock on a door.

How to pray for non-Christians
- That the Holy Spirit will prepare their hearts.
- That the Holy Spirit will remove the veil from their hearts.
  See 2 Corinthians 3:12-16.

Don't forget that you're fighting a spiritual war
The devil will do everything he can to stop you from witnessing for Jesus.

Paul often spoke about Christians being caught up in a spiritual fight. He said,

"our struggle is not against flesh and blood,
but against the rulers,
against the authorities,
against the powers of this dark world
and against the spiritual forces of evil
in the heavenly realms."

That's why he told them: "Therefore put on the full armor of God."
(See Ephesians 6:11-12).

Pray for those you have lead to the Lord

Anyone who has been helped by you to accept Christ has a very special spiritual link with you. So you have a responsibility to pray for them.

The apostle Paul called himself a father to those he had led to Christ, and he called the people he led to Christ his sons (children).

1. Timothy

"To Timothy my true *son* in the faith." *1 Timothy 1:2*
"My *son*, I give you this instruction." *1 Timothy 1:18*
"To Timothy, my dear *son*." *2 Timothy 1:2*
"My *son*, be strong in the grace that is in Christ Jesus." *2 Timothy 2:1*

2. Christians at Corinth

"Even though you have ten thousand guardians in Christ, you do not have many fathers, for in Christ Jesus I became your *father* in the gospel." *1 Corinthians 4:15*

3. Onesimus (a converted runaway slave)

"I appeal to you for my *son* Onesimus, who became my *son* while I was in chains." *Philemon 10*

4. Titus

"To Titus, my true *son* in our common faith." *Titus 1:4*

See also: *Don't ever forget the Holy Spirit*, pages 56-57.

The bridge

QUOTATION FROM A FAITHFUL SOUL WINNER TO SET YOU THINKING

"I look upon this world as a wrecked vessel. God has given me a lifeboat and said to me: 'Moody, save all you can.'" *D.L. Moody.*

The bridge to God

There are many different illustrations you can use as you share Jesus. One helpful idea is the concept of a bridge.

A good question to ask someone who entertains doubts about Jesus and about why he died on the cross is as follows:

Question: "If you could climb to heaven under your own power, why then would God allow Jesus to suffer and sacrifice his life?"

Answer: "God sent Jesus as a bridge between us and God. The bridge was in the shape of a cross spanning the gap between earth and heaven."

Four steps

There are four steps for a non-Christian to take in order to cross over this bridge to God. The four steps are four ideas or truths he/she needs to accept.

Step 1: to cross the bridge
God loves us and has a great plan for our lives.
- Read together a verse about God's love. *John 3:16.*

Step 2: to cross the bridge
Our sin separates us from God so we can't experience God's plan and love for us. Our sin makes a tremendously wide gap, as it were, between us and God.
- Read together a verse about God's love. *Romans 3:23; 6:23.*

Step 3: to cross the bridge
God sent Jesus to bridge the gap between us and God. Jesus did this when he died on the cross for our sins.
- Read together a verse about God's love. *Romans 5:8*

Step 4: to cross the bridge
Step four is to actually cross over the bridge. We do this by allowing Jesus into our lives as our friend and Savior.
- Read together a verse about God's love. *John 1:12; 3:3-5; Titus 3:5.*

Informal missionaries

Adolf Harnack, in his massive book, *The Mission and Expansion of Christianity*, wrote: "We cannot hesitate to believe that the great mission of Christianity was accomplished by means of informal missionaries."

All Christians are "informal" missionaries in this sense.

Time to get tough

John the Baptist and the blunt approach

John the Baptist believed in the direct approach to personal evangelism. Wherever he went he seemed to shoot from the hip! Some people seem to have the gift of being able to boldly engage people and then speak about Jesus. You may not be able to do this, but you can pray for those who can.

John's message: "Repent."

• To crowds of ordinary people

John's message to them was: "Repent, for the kingdom of heaven is near." *Matthew 3:1*
The result: They confessed their sins, "and were baptized by him [John] in the Jordan River." *Matthew 3:6*

• To top religious leaders

John called the Pharisees and Sadducees, "You brood of vipers!" *Matthew 3:7*
John's message to them was: "Produce fruit in keeping with repentance. And do not think that you can say to yourselves, 'We have Abraham as our father.'" *Matthew 3:9*

Peter's message: "Repent."

• To those who had crucified Christ

Peter's message to those who recognized their sinfulness and "were cut to the heart" was, "Repent and be baptized, every one of you ..." *Acts 2:38*
The result: "Those who accepted his message were baptized, and about three thousand were added to their number that day." *Acts 2:41*

Key verse about John the Baptist's witness to Jesus

John the Baptist said, "He [Jesus] must become greater, I must decrease." *John :3:30*

See also: *Softly, softly*, pages 44-45; *The importance of preaching*, pages 60-61.

Five ways not to share your faith

1. Keep on talking about yourself.
2. If you're asked something you don't know, pretend you do know!
3. Give the impression that you are superior to the person you are talking to.
4. Never talk about Jesus.
5. Allow yourself to be sidetracked by diversionary tactics.

HOW TO SHARE YOUR FAITH
Hot tip No 4:

Don't procrastinate because it is such tough work. Remember: you are helping to lead people to a righteous, sin-forgiven life.

"Those who are wise will shine like the brightness of the heavens, and those who lead many to righteousness, like the stars for ever and ever." *Daniel 12:3*

Five handy things to remember

1. Only *God* converts anyone.
2. Remember the things that helped you to become a Christian.
3. Ask someone else to pray for you before you share your faith.
4. Attend a course with other Christians on How to Share Your Faith.
5. Remember who Jesus is: that will help you to focus on him.

Softly, softly

Start where people are

Don't use the same approach with everyone you meet. Find out where people are in their spiritual understanding and start there. Some people are acutely aware of a sense of guilt, others are lonely, or feel that life is meaningless.

It's pointless spending countless hours covering the arguments for the existence of God with someone who has no problems over God's existence.

Q. Did Jesus have a purpose in telling the parables of the lost coin, the lost sheep and the lost son?

A. Definitely. Jesus had a special insight into the spiritual condition of everyone he met. But he used this insight to ensure that he applied an aspect of the gospel which was most appropriate for that person.

"Now the tax collectors and 'sinners' were all gathering around to hear him. But the Pharisees and the teachers of the law muttered, 'This man welcomes sinners and eats with them.' Then Jesus told them this parable."
Luke 15:1-3

The three famous parables of the lost coin, the lost sheep and the prodigal son were told against the background of the resentment that the top religious leaders had towards the way Jesus mixed with ordinary people.

Spiritual hints about sharing your faith

Pray
And what should you pray for?
a. Ask for the Holy Spirit to help you.
"So he said to me, 'This is the word of the Lord to Zerubbabel: Not by might, nor by power, but by my Spirit,' says the Lord Almighty." *Zechariah 4:6*

b. Ask for boldness.
"The wicked man flees though no one pursues, but the righteous are as bold as a lion." *Proverbs 28:1*
c. Be soul-conscious
Do you have a prayer list of people who are not Christians that you are regularly praying for?

Some practical hints

If you go visiting at a person's home, here are some practical hints.

1. Your dress. Don't draw attention to yourself.
2. Your breath. Take some breath mints with you.
3. Your cleanliness. Take a shower before you go!
4. Take a Bible or New Testament with you.
5. Go armed with literature you may wish to leave behind.
6. Go in twos. It is safer. You can pray together and encourage each other, and learn from each other. That's how Jesus sent out his disciples. "After this the Lord appointed seventy-two others and sent them *two by two* ahead of him to every town and place where he was about to go." *Luke 10:1*
7. When you are in somebody's home, you are a guest. Don't argue. Be pleasant and courteous.

I failed!

"Christ sent me to preach the gospel and he will look after the results."
Mary Slessor

Success versus faithfulness

Jesus never said that everyone would respond in a positive way when they hear the gospel. So don't be discouraged when you spend a whole evening knocking on doors or an afternoon visiting a hospital ward and no one seems to be interested in Jesus. What matters is that we are faithful, not that we are successful.

And if you are successful ...

A word of warning. When the seventy-two disciples returned to Jesus they were full of joy and said, "Lord, even the demons submit to us in your name." But Jesus, rather surprisingly, replied, "Do not rejoice that the spirits submit to you, but rejoice that your names are written in heaven." *Luke 10:17, 20*

So we don't rejoice in our success, but rejoice in the fact that people are coming to know Jesus.

Jesus and the rich young man

"Now a man came up to Jesus and asked, 'Teacher, what good thing must I do to get eternal life?'

'Why do you ask me about what is good?' Jesus replied. 'There is only One who is good. If you want to enter life, obey the commandments.'

'Which ones?' the man inquired. Jesus replied, '"Do not murder, do not commit adultery, do not steal, do not give false testimony, honor your father and mother," and "love your neighbor as yourself."'

'All these I have kept,' the young man said. 'What do I still lack?' Jesus answered, 'If you want to be perfect, go, sell your possessions and give to the poor, and you will have treasure in heaven. Then come, follow me.'

When the young man heard this, he went away sad, because he had great wealth."

Matthew 19:16-22

What went wrong?

The rich young man did many things that we would say were right.

1. He went to the right person – Jesus. *Matthew 19:16*

2. He went in the right frame of mind – he "fell on his knees" before Jesus. *See Mark 10:17*

3. He asked the right question – how to find "eternal life." *Matthew 19:16*

But it all ended in tears! The young man is the only person in the Gospels who is recorded as having left Jesus "sad."

So did Jesus fail?

"The young man ... went away sad." That doesn't sound much like a success story.

Clearly, since Jesus was the Son of God, he did not do anything wrong here or anywhere else.

Visibly, the love of money gripped this young man's heart.

This young man was jolted into seeing the stark choice he had to make between following Jesus and following something else. All we can do is simply present this choice.

What about children?

Children and evangelism

Many people are more tongue-tied about introducing Jesus to children than they are to adults. Don't let anybody deceive you into feeling that children are too young to become followers of Jesus.

The example of Jesus

In Jesus' day, children not only had no rights, they were often so overlooked that they were made to feel that they hardly counted.

So Jesus' attitude to children was most remarkable.

Mark 10:13-16

Verse 13	"People were bringing little children to Jesus to have him touch them, but the disciples rebuked them.
Verse 14	When Jesus saw this, he was indignant. He said to them, 'Let the little children come to me, and do not hinder them, for the kingdom of God belongs to such as these.
Verse 15	I tell you the truth, anyone who will not receive the kingdom of God like a little child will never enter it.'
Verse 16	And he took the children in his arms, put his hands on them and blessed them."

Points to note

1. Ordinary people expected Jesus to help children in a spiritual way – *verse 13*.
2. The disciples wanted to brush the children to one side – *verse 13*.
3. Jesus was not indifferent to children but he was "indignant" toward those disciples with wrong attitudes – *verse 14*.

4. We have Jesus' specific command concerning child evangelism – "Let the little children come to me" – *verse 14*.
5. Jesus loved children and blessed them – *verse 16*.

The Wordless Book

You can make your own wordless book to use with children. Here is how it could be used.

"Hi! Have you ever seen a book with no words in it?

Here's my book which has no words. Watch out for the different colors. Each color tells a story.

Gold page

This gold page stands for heaven. The streets of heaven are made of pure gold.

Jesus has gone to heaven to prepare a place for each of his friends.

In heaven there will be no more crying, no more sadness and no more illness.

Dark page

The dark page is a sad page. It reminds us of our sin. It helps us remember anything that we have done or anything that we have said or anything that we have thought which did not please God.

Red page

This red page is both a sad page and a happy page.

It is a sad page because it reminds us of Jesus dying on the cross.

It is a happy page because it reminds us that Jesus died so our sins can be forgiven.

White page

This clean page is your page in this story.

It stands for the moment we ask Jesus to be our special friend and accept him as our Savior.

Green cover

Did you notice the color of the cover of the book?

The green cover of my wordless book reminds me to grow. Jesus is happy if we desire to grow and be more like him.

These are the five colors of my wordless book. Each color has a secret story. See if you can remember what each one is."

There are so many oddballs and fanatics around

Who says who is an oddball ?

Is an oddball someone carrying a sandwich board proclaiming: "The end of the world is nigh"? Many would say that you are an oddball for reading a book like this.

Beware of judging other Christians and writing them off: "Do not judge, or you too will be judged" *Matthew 7:1*.

Some would say that anyone who engages in personal evangelism is a fanatic. Occasionally there will be people who are far from being mentally stable and who attach themselves to a Christian fellowship. Rather than being a reason for embarrassment – that should be a reason to rejoice that such people find help within a Christian group.

They don't belong to us/our church

Beware of rejecting the ministry and gospel proclamation of other Christians. Remember that Jesus said: "Whoever is not against us is for us."

"'Teacher,' said John, 'we saw a man driving out demons in your name and we told him to stop, because he was not one of us.' 'Do not stop him,' Jesus said. 'No one who does a miracle in my name can in the next moment say anything bad about me, for whoever is not against us is for us. I tell you the truth, anyone who gives you a cup of water in my name because you belong to Christ will certainly not lose his reward.'" *Mark 9:38-41*.

HOW TO SHARE YOUR FAITH
Hot tip No 5:
Don't worry if you are labeled as an oddball.
Paul was pronounced insane by Festus. "Festus interrupted Paul's defense. 'You are out of your mind, Paul!' he exclaimed. 'Your great learning is driving you insane.'"
Acts 26:24.

Witnessing for Jesus is a serious business

Read through Matthew 13:36-43	**Lessons to learn about witnessing**
Verse 36	Then he left the crowd and went into the house. His disciples came to him and said, "Explain to us the parable of the weeds in the field."	1. Seek wisdom from Jesus
Verse 37	He answered, "The one who sowed the good seed is the Son of Man."	2. We must work with Jesus 3. We must believe that the Bible is good
Verse 38	"The field is the world, and the good seed stands for the sons of the kingdom. The weeds are the sons of the evil one,"	4. There is no limit to where we should witness
Verse 39	"and the enemy who sows them is the devil. The harvest is the end of the age, and the harvesters are angels."	5. We must never underestimate Satan's power 6. We must remember that there will be a harvest
Verses 40-42	"As the weeds are pulled up and burned in the fire, so it will be at the end of the age. The Son of Man will send out his angels, and they will weed out of his kingdom everything that causes sin and all who do evil. They will throw them into the fiery furnace, where there will be weeping and gnashing of teeth."	7. We must remember what will happen to the wicked
Verse 43	"Then the righteous will shine like the sun in the kingdom of their Father. He who has ears, let him hear."	8. We must always be grateful for our salvation in Jesus

I'm no good at speaking

Excuses, excuses, excuses!

If we all waited until we thought that we were fully equipped to share our faith, no personal evangelism would ever take place.

"I'm not a good speaker," is a favorite excuse. But don't worry, if God wants you to be a good speaker either in public or on a one-to-one basis, *he* will equip you.

Remember Moses?

Read through Exodus 3:11–4:12.

- God was appointing Moses to lead his people out of Egypt.
  Exodus 3:12

- Moses' complaint – "I'm not a good speaker."
  "Moses said to the Lord, 'O Lord, I have never been eloquent, neither in the past nor since you have spoken to your servant. I am slow of speech and of tongue.'" *Exodus 4:10*

- The Lord's reply – "I will teach you."
  "The Lord said to him [Moses], 'Who gave man his mouth? Who makes him deaf or mute? Who gives him sight or makes him blind? Is it not I, the Lord? Now go; I will help you speak and will teach you what to say.'"
  Exodus 4:11-12

Remember Paul?

Paul was a theological elitist. He went to the best Bible college of his day. He was one of the leading theologians among the Jews, and became perhaps the greatest Christian thinker, theologian and missionary strategist of all time.

But he was conscious of his *weakness*! He knew that sharing Jesus was always a spiritual battle. So he always remained fully aware of his own human weakness but relied totally on God's spiritual power.

"When I am *weak*, then I am strong."
2 Corinthians 12:10

"I can do everything through him [Jesus] who gives me strength."
Philippians 4:13

The Roman road to salvation

Here's how the outline of the gospel can be simply explained from Paul's wonderful letter to the Romans.

1. A sinner has a problem – the sin problem

a. Romans says we have all sinned.

"There is no one righteous, not even one." *Romans 3:10 See also Romans 3:23*

b. Romans says that spiritual death is the result of unforgiven sin.

"For the wages of sin is death, but the gift of God is eternal life in Christ Jesus our Lord." *Romans 6:23*

2. The solution to the sin problem

Romans says God has provided the way out for sinners.

"But God demonstrates his own love for us in this: While we were still sinners, Christ died for us." *Romans 5:8. See also Romans 5:12; Romans 2:4*

3. The action a sinner must take

a. Romans says a sinner must accept Jesus as Savior.

"That if you confess with your mouth; 'Jesus is Lord,' and believe in your heart that God raised him from the dead, you will be saved." *Romans 10:9*

b. Romans says that new believers then re-enact the death, burial and resurrection through baptism.

"Or don't you know that all of us who were baptized into Christ Jesus were baptized into his death? We were therefore buried with him through baptism to death in order that, just as Christ was raised from the dead ... we too may live a new life." *Romans 6:3-4*

Opportunity knocks

Learning how to do it

One of the best ways to learn about sharing our faith in Jesus with others is to see how the first followers of Jesus did this.

Read through Acts 8:26-40 to see what it teaches you about leading a person to Jesus.

Acts 8:26-40

26 Now an angel of the Lord said to Philip, "Go south to the road – the desert road – that goes down from Jerusalem to Gaza."	Philip was open to God's leading. Philip had just been involved in preaching the gospel to crowds of people in a city. Now he obeyed the Lord and went off to the desert. *See Acts 8:4-7.*
27 So he started out, and on his way he met an Ethiopian eunuch, an important official in charge of all the treasury of Candace, queen of the Ethiopians. This man had gone to Jerusalem to worship,	Wealth and an important job did not satisfy the spiritual longing of this government official.
28 and on his way home was sitting in his chariot reading the book of Isaiah the prophet.	The Bible is the best book to use in sharing your faith. This man was already reading it!
29 The Spirit told Philip, "Go to that chariot and stay near it."	Philip was alert to the Spirit. Philip obeyed even if he may not have known why he had to run alongside this chariot.
30 Then Philip ran up to the chariot and heard the man reading Isaiah the prophet. "Do you understand what you are reading?" Philip asked.	Philip did not beat about the bush. He asked a question. He wanted to find out what spiritual understanding the Ethiopian had.
31 "How can I," he said, "unless someone explains it to me?" So he invited Philip to come up and sit with him.	Philip used this God-given opportunity and jumped up into the chariot. You can lead a person to Jesus, no matter where you are.

32 The eunuch was reading this passage of Scripture: "He was led like a sheep to the slaughter, and as a lamb before the shearer is silent, so he did not open his mouth.

33 In his humiliation he was deprived of justice. Who can speak of his descendants? For his life was taken from the earth."

34 The eunuch asked Philip, "Tell me, please, who is the prophet talking about, himself or someone else?"

The Ethiopian was in a bit of a quandary, for he clearly did not understand what he was reading. But he wanted someone to help him.

---

35 Then Philip began with that very passage of Scripture and told him the good news about Jesus.

Philip used the Bible to explain to him about the good news of Jesus.

---

36 As they traveled along the road, they came to some water and the eunuch said, "Look, here is water. Why shouldn't I be baptized?"

38 And he gave orders to stop the chariot. Then both Philip and the eunuch went down into the water and Philip baptized him.

The Ethiopian opened his heart to Jesus. *(Verse 37 is a footnote in many Bibles, because it only comes in late manuscripts. It is a wonderful testimony of faith in Jesus. "Philip said, 'If you believe with all your heart, you may.' The eunuch answered, 'I believe that Jesus Christ is the Son of God.'")* Philip baptized the Ethiopian there and then. Baptism was the first response after he accepted Christ.

---

39 When they came up out of the water, the Spirit of the Lord suddenly took Philip away, and the eunuch did not see him again, but went on his way rejoicing.

Philip continued to be open to the Spirit of the Lord. Somebody else would have to provide follow-up for the new Ethiopian Christian. The Ethiopian rejoiced in Jesus.

---

40 Philip, however, appeared at Azotus and traveled about, preaching the gospel in all the towns until he reached Caesarea.

Philip carried on being faithful in serving Jesus.

A golden verse

Acts 8:35 is one of the most helpful verses in the Bible about how to lead a person to Jesus. Memorize it. Ask God to help you to follow it when you share your faith.

Don't ever forget the Holy Spirit

"There is no better evangelist in the world than the Holy Spirit."
D.L. Moody

Who gives spiritual life?

Answer: Only the Holy Spirit. Work done trusting in human efforts gives no spiritual life. Work done trusting in the Holy Spirit is work done for eternity.

Jesus stated this key principle: "Flesh gives birth to flesh, but the Spirit gives birth to spirit." *John 3:6.*

The work of the Holy Spirit in John's gospel

What the Holy Spirit does	Quotation	Bible reference
1. He gives spiritual life	"The Spirit gives life."	*John 6:63*
2. He lives inside believers	"He lives with you and will be in you."	*John 14:17; Romans 8:9*
3. He witnesses to Jesus	"He will testify about me."	*John 15:26*
4. He honors and praises Jesus	"He will bring glory to me."	*John 16:14*
5. He convicts people about sin	"When he comes, he will convict the world of guilt in regard to sin and righteousness and judgment: in regard to sin, because men do not believe in me; in regard to righteousness, because I am going to the Father, where you can see me no longer; and in regard to judgment, because the prince of this world now stands condemned."	*John 16:8-11*
6. He convicts people about righteousness		*John 16:8-11*
7. He convicts people about judgment		*John 16:8-11*

No preparation needed?

There is one kind of occasion when Jesus said we should not try to work out in advance how to witness for him.

It is during any kind of persecution. Then, "you will be given what to say."

> "Be on your guard against men; they will hand you over to the local councils and flog you in their synagogues. On my account you will be brought before governors and kings as witnesses to them and to the Gentiles. But when they arrest you, do not worry about what to say or how to say it. At that time you will be given what to say, for it will not be you speaking, but the Spirit of your Father speaking through you."
> *Matthew 10:17-20.*

Of course this means that we should never be surprised when persecution comes our way. We are never left on our own to witness as the Holy Spirit promises to be with us all the time.

A word of warning

Don't expect too much too soon from a new Christian. Different people grow and develop at different rates, both physically and spiritually.

Don't give a new Christian the impression that he has to keep a whole list of new rules such as:

1. Do this …
2. Do this …
3. Do this …
4. Don't do this …
5. Don't do this …
6. Don't do this …

There's really only one important thing: *to develop his/her friendship with Jesus.*

QUOTATION FROM A FAITHFUL SOUL WINNER TO SET YOU THINKING

"One loving soul sets another on fire."
Augustine of Hippo.

The power of a Christ-like life

"His disciples have to look more saved if I am to believe in the Savior."
Nietzche

Where was the name "Christian" first used?

It first occurs in the Acts of the Apostles. Barnabas and Paul met with and taught the Christians in this place for a year.

Then, "the disciples were called Christians first at Antioch." *Acts 11:26*

They turned the world upside down for Jesus

While Christians rejoiced over the "the spread of the gospel," non-Christians referred to this evangelism as "trouble".

"These men who have caused trouble all over the world have now come here." *Acts 17:6*

Divine power

Luke's record in the Acts of the Apostles shows how Christians turned the world upside down.

They were the first to say that it was only through the power of Jesus in their lives.

The following verses describe what happened to Peter and John after they had been illegally locked in prison for the night.

They knew that they had been with Jesus

1. It was quite a gathering

2. Where do Christians find their power?

3. They kept on being filled with the Holy Spirit

4. They kept Jesus at the center of their witness

5. They always linked Jesus and salvation

6. Others saw that they had been with the risen Jesus

58

Letting the light of Jesus shine

Jesus once said: "Let your light shine before men, that they may see your good deeds and praise your Father in heaven." *Matthew 5:16*

Jesus was dead and buried, but his followers still knew him as he was alive in the Spirit.

"The next day the rulers, elders and teachers of the law met in Jerusalem. Annas the high priest was there, and so were Caiaphas, John, Alexander and the other men of the high priest's family." *Acts 4:5-6*

"They had Peter and John brought before them and began to question them: 'By what power or what name did you do this?'" *Acts 4:7*

"Then Peter, filled with the Holy Spirit, said to them: 'Rulers and elders of the people! If we are being called to account today for an act of kindness shown to a cripple and are asked how he was healed, then know this, you and all the people of Israel:'" *Acts 4:8-10*

"It is by the name of Jesus Christ of Nazareth, whom you crucified but whom God raised from the dead, that this man stands before you healed. He is '"the stone you builders rejected, which has become the capstone."'" *Acts 4:10-11*

"Salvation is found in no one else, for there is no other name under heaven given to men by which we must be saved." *Acts 4:12*

"When they saw the courage of Peter and John and realized that they were unschooled, ordinary men, they were astonished and they took note that *these men had been with Jesus*." *Acts 4:13*

The importance of preaching

"Millions have never heard the name of Jesus. Hundreds of millions have seen a missionary only once in their lives, and know nothing of our King. Shall we let them perish? Can we go to our beds and sleep while China, India, Japan, and other nations are being damned? Are we clear of their blood? Have they no claim upon us? We ought to put it on this footing –

not 'Can I prove that I *ought* to go?'
but 'Can I prove that I *ought not* to go?'
C.H. Spurgeon

One-on-one witnessing and preaching
You could adapt the above quote and say, "Millions have never had the way of salvation explained to them on a one-on-one basis."

The priority of preaching
Preaching about the Lord is extremely important in most churches and denominations, but for some churches it is out of style and not fashionable.

The apostle Paul was clear about its permanent importance.

"'Everyone who calls on the name of the Lord will be saved.' How, then, can they call on the one they have not believed in? And how can they believe in the one of whom they have not heard? And how can they hear without someone *preaching* to them? And how can they preach unless they are sent? As it is written, 'How beautiful are the feet of those who bring good news.'" *Romans 10:13-15*

There will never be an overabundance of Christian preachers in God's church.

Making use of sermons
- Invite someone to an evangelistic service or special preaching meeting.
- Lend a cassette of a good gospel sermon to a friend.

A ten point charter for Christian witnessing

1.	Why we do it	*Romans 1:14*
2.	Our special prayer	*Matthew 9:38*
3.	Our special helper	*Philippians 4:13*
4.	Our point of focus	*John 3:16*
5.	Our reward	*1 Thessalonains 2:19-20*
6.	Our power	"But you will receive power when the Holy Spirit comes on you; and you will be my witnesses in Jerusalem, and in all Judea and Samaria, and to the ends of the earth." *Acts 1:8*
7.	Our message	*Romans 1:16*
8.	Our cutting edge	*2 Timothy 4:2*
9.	Our moment to speak	*2 Corinthians 6:2*
10.	A great example	*Mark 5:19-20*

You are unique

"The gospel does not fall from the clouds like rain by accident, but is brought by the hands of men and women to whom God has sent it."
John Calvin

Some sobering facts

• You may be the only Christian some of your family and friends know.

• Many religious people and, probably, many of your co-workers and friends have never had the actual good news of Jesus presented to them.

Where should I begin?
Start where you are!

"As Jesus was getting into the boat, the man who had been demon-possessed begged to go with him. Jesus did not let him, but said, 'Go home to your family and tell them how much the Lord has done for you, and how he has had mercy on you.'" *Mark 5:18-19*

Many people find that their families are the hardest people to witness to. But Jesus told this new disciple that that was where he had to start.

"But I'm not as gifted as many other people"

Don't worry about how many gifts and talents you have. Put to work the ones you do have.

Read the parable of the talents from *Matthew 25:14-30*.

Note that the three people in the story were given a *different number of talents*. In the parable, the person who used his five talents and the person who used his two talents were commended with the same words:

"'Well done, good and faithful servant! You have been faithful with a few things; I will put you in charge of many things.'" *Matthew 25:21 and 23*

In the parable the person who was condemned was the one who had been given one talent. Why? Because he did not bother to use it. He just hid it in the ground.

Chosen by God

To complain about our lack of gifts is to come close to insulting our Creator. Think about what you do possess:

a. You were chosen by God before the world was created.

"For he chose us in him before the creation of the world."
Ephesians 1:4

b. You are chosen to be God's ambassador.

"We are therefore Christ's *ambassadors*, as though God were making his appeal through us. We implore on Christ's behalf: Be reconciled to God."
2 Corinthians 5:20

c. It is Jesus' wish that you should be fruitful.

"I am the vine; you are the branches. If a man remains in me and I in him, he will bear much fruit; apart from me you can do nothing." *John 15:5*

Stardom versus obscurity

There is a tendency in some Christian circles to place on a pedestal the famous people who have become Christians, especially if they are famous sports personalities or well-known entertainers.

How different that is from the early days of Christianity. Here Paul is writing to encourage the Christians at Corinth to remember who they were in the eyes of the world when God called them into his kingdom.

"Brothers, think of what you were when you were called. Not many of you were wise by human standards; not many were influential; not many were of noble birth. But God chose the foolish things of the world to shame the wise; God chose the weak things of the world to shame the strong. He chose the lowly things of this world and the despised things – and the things that are not – to nullify the things that are, so that no one may boast before him." *1 Corinthians 1:26-29*

Using the Internet

What's the point in using the Internet?

1. The person you are trying to help can follow the steps to faith in Jesus at his/her own speed.
2. He/she can do this when it is most convenient to him/her.
3. This can be done in privacy.
4. The best evangelistic sites on the Internet are easy to follow.
5. These Internet sites have been compiled by dedicated Christian evangelists and evangelistic organizations. Their teaching is probably clearer than anything most other Christians can manage.

How is the Internet used in personal evangelism?

Just give a list of the following sites to your friend or e-mail them to him/her.

http://www.grahamassn.org/ bgea/bgeasal/bgeastps.htm

This site and the other three mentioned on this page were set up by the Billy Graham Evangelistic Association.

This one introduces a person to Jesus. It is called *Steps to peace with God*.

http://www.grahamassn.org/ bgea/bgeasal/follow.htm

This site is ideal for a brand new Christian. It even has a follow up letter from Billy Graham.

http://www.grahamassn.org/ bgea/bgeasal/salmain.htm

This site contains answers to some of the most frequently asked questions about the Christian faith.

http://www.gospelcom.net

This site lists over one hundred Christian organizations that can provide help and assistance in growing as a Christian.

Knowing
God's Will
made easier

Some Christians become completely paralyzed when it comes to thinking about God's will for their lives.

To start with it seems a mighty presumption to think that the Creator of the universe is interested in me and my little life.

Then there's the problem of "How on earth am I expected to find out exactly what God's will for me is, anyway?"

And then there's another problem. Even if I was 100% certain about God's will for me, would I want to follow it?

Maybe after reading *Knowing God's will made easier* we'll find it possible to agree with Billy Graham when he said, "We do not understand the intricate pattern of the stars in their courses, but we know that He who created them does, and that just as surely as He guides them, He is charting a safe course for us."

If you know and follow God's will, you are bound to be a dynamic Christian.

Contents

4

There's no secret formula to discover

No special button to press

Finding out about God's will is not like logging on to the Internet and pressing an icon labeled "Knowing God's Will," which will then display everything you want to know.

In the Bible, God has given us a number of general principles for guidance. We are expected to know what these are and to follow them. There are dozens of such principles. Here are just two of them.

Ask

Do you lack wisdom? Here is God's remedy to that: "Ask!"

"If any of you lacks wisdom, he should ask God, who gives generously to all without finding fault, and it will be given to him." *James 1:5*

Ask as if you mean it!

Jesus stressed that people should be in earnest when they prayed: "So I say to you: ask and it will be given to you; seek and you will find; knock and the door will be opened to you. For everyone who asks receives; he who seeks finds; and to him who knocks, the door will be opened." *Luke 11:9-10*

Why shouldn't we ask for signs – Gideon did?

Gideon puts God to the test

"Gideon said to God, 'If you will save Israel by my hand as you have promised – look, I will place a wool fleece on the threshing-floor. If there is dew only on the fleece and all the ground is dry, then I will know that you will save Israel by my hand, as you said.' And this is what happened. Gideon rose early the next day; he squeezed the fleece and wrung out the dew – a bowlful of water.

Then Gideon said to God, 'Do not be angry with me. Let me make just one more request. Allow me one more test with the fleece. This time make the fleece dry and the ground covered with dew.' That night God did so. Only the fleece was dry; all the ground was covered with dew." *Judges 6:36-40*

What is the Bible telling us?

When you read Bible stories, ask yourself whether they are giving a warning to heed, or an example to follow.

The Bible tells us about both the good and the bad sides of Gideon's character.

Gideon's good points
- He was humble. "I am the least in my family." *Judges 6:15*
- He obeyed God. "Gideon ... did as the LORD told him." *Judges 6:27*
- He experienced God's Spirit. "The Spirit of the LORD came upon Gideon." *Judges 6:34*
- He was a clever strategist. *Judges 7:16-18*
- He was diplomatic. *Judges 8:1-3*

Gideon's bad points
- Gideon was not content with the first miracle, a wet fleece on a dry background. He had to ask for a second (and more difficult) miracle, a dry fleece on a wet background.
- It looks as if Gideon himself knew that what he was doing was wrong. He said, "Do not be angry with me."

Gideon showed great courage and served God faithfully in many ways. But this does not mean to say he never did anything wrong. His whole story is told in Judges 6–8.

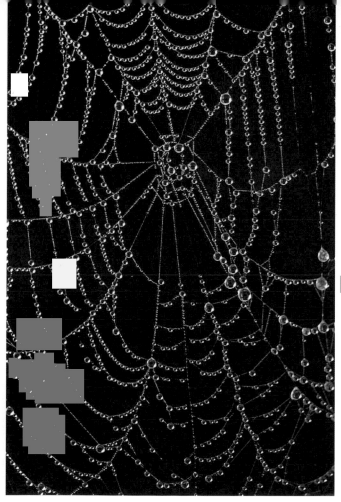

Jesus condemns people seeking a sign

When Jesus went preaching and healing, instead of believing in him, some people asked for a sign that he was the Son of God. Jesus said, "This is a wicked generation. It asks for a miraculous sign, but none will be given it except the sign of Jonah."
Luke 11:29

How does the Bible say God guides us?

The Old Testament

The Old Testament gives many examples of people who were guided by God in a variety of ways.

Person	Incident	Bible reference
Abraham	God sends Abraham to Canaan	*Genesis 12*
Abraham's servant	The servant looks for a suitable wife for Isaac	*Genesis 24*
Jacob	God shows Jacob how to take the best goats from Laban	*Genesis 31*
God's people	God provides a pillar of fire to guide the people in the desert	*Exodus 13:21*
Joshua	God guides Joshua through sacred lots	*Joshua 18:10*
God's people	God provides prophets to tell the people his will	*Deuteronomy 18:14-19*
Saul	Saul uses lots to discover who has broken the fast	*1 Samuel 14:41-43*

The New Testament

People in the New Testament were guided by God in "supernatural" ways.

Person	Incident	Bible reference
Joseph	God tells Joseph, in a dream, to escape to Egypt	*Matthew 2:13-15*
Philip	An angel tells Philip to go to the desert road	*Acts 8:26-40*
Cornelius	God speaks to Cornelius in a vision	*Acts 10:1-8*
Peter	God speaks to Peter through a trance, as he prays	*Acts 10:9-23*
Pilate's wife	God warns Pilate's wife through a disturbing dream	*Matthew 27:19*
Church leaders	The Holy Spirit guides the Council at Jerusalem	*Acts 15:1-29*

An angel directs Philip to the treasurer of Candace

"Now an angel of the Lord said to Philip, 'Go south to the road – the desert road – that goes down from Jerusalem to Gaza.' So he started out, and on his way he met an Ethiopian eunuch, an important official in charge of all the treasury of Candace, Queen of the Ethiopians. ... Philip ... told him the good news about Jesus ... and baptized him. When they came up out of the water, the Spirit of the Lord suddenly took Philip away, and the eunuch did not see him again, but went on his way rejoicing."
Acts 8:26-27, 35, 38-39

What can stop me from knowing God's will?

Warnings in the Old Testament

• Deliberate sin
"If I cherished sin in my heart,
  the Lord would not have
    listened;
but God has surely listened
  and heard my voice in prayer."
Psalm 66:18-19

• Turning a deaf ear to people in need
"If a man shuts his ears to the cry
  of the poor,
  he too will cry out and not be
    answered."
Proverbs 21:13

• Ignoring God's teaching
"If anyone turns a deaf ear to the
  law,
even his prayers are detestable."
Proverbs 28:9

• Active participation in evil
"The eyes of the LORD are on the
  righteous
  and his ears are attentive to their
    cry;
the face of the LORD is against
  those who do evil,
  to cut off the memory of them
    from the earth."
Psalm 34:15-16

James

James points out four things to avoid if we want to know God's will and serve him in the right way.

• Failing to ask God
"You do not have, because you do
not ask God." *James 4:2*

• Asking in the wrong way
"You do not receive, because you
ask with wrong motives, that you
may spend what you get on your
pleasures." *James 4:2-3*

• Having doubts that God gives generously
"But when he asks, he must
believe and not doubt, because he
who doubts is like a wave of the
sea, blown and tossed by the
wind. That man should not think
he will receive anything from the
Lord." *James 1:6-7*

• Asking in a proud way
"God opposes the proud but gives
grace to the humble." *James 4:6;
quoting Proverbs 3:34*

Jesus teaches about prayer

• Have a forgiving spirit
Jesus taught that in order to receive forgiveness, we must forgive. This principle also applies to prayer and to seeking God's will. "For if you forgive men when they sin against you, your heavenly Father will also forgive you. But if you do not forgive men their sins, your Father will not forgive your sins." *Matthew 6:14-15*

• Make it up with people before you pray to God
"Therefore, if you are offering your gift at the altar and there remember that your brother has something against you, leave your gift there in front of the altar. First go and be reconciled to your brother; then come and offer your gift." *Matthew 5:23-24*

Trusting God does not mean we don't need friends!

Iron sharpens iron
"As iron sharpens iron, so one man sharpens another."
Proverbs 27:17

The apostle Paul is comforted
It is instructive to see how the "super-spiritual" apostle Paul was once comforted by God. Was it through a vision? Was it through prayer? Was it through a miraculous event? Or did God comfort Paul through a worship service?

No doubt God did "speak" to Paul in these ways, but Paul was also comforted by a Christian friend. He was anxiously waiting for news about the Christians at Corinth. Paul writes, "God, who comforts the downcast, comforted us by the coming of Titus." *2 Corinthians 7:6*

For Paul, there was no conflict in trusting God and being comforted by a friend.

Characteristics of a good friend
The Book of Proverbs advises us to choose our friends carefully.

"A righteous man is cautious in friendship."
Proverbs 12:26

"He who walks with the wise grows wise,
   but a companion of fools suffers harm."
Proverbs 13:20

It may be that you can be a friend to someone who is seeking God's guidance for his or her life.

Friends found in the Book of Proverbs
• Loyal friends   *Proverbs 17:17; 27:10*
• Trusted friends   *Proverbs 27:6*
• A special friend   *Proverbs 18:24*

Jesus is a friend
- "You are my friends if you do what I command." *John 15:14*
- "I no longer call you servants. ... Instead, I have called you friends." *John 15:15*

God as a friend
- "The LORD would speak to Moses face to face, as a man speaks with his friend." *Exodus 33:11*

See also: *Key 7: Ask a friend*, page 28

Nine keys to finding God's will

Nine keys
Pages 16-33 give nine keys to finding God's will.

Checklist

- [ ] Key 1: Be humble. [ ]
- [ ] Key 2: Pray. [ ]
- [ ] Key 3: Follow the light you already have. [ ]
- [ ] Key 4: Don't give up. [ ]
- [ ] Key 5: Don't be put off by barriers. [ ]
- [ ] Key 6: Use your mind. [ ]
- [ ] Key 7: Ask a friend. [ ]
- [ ] Key 8: Remember, God is not in a hurry. [ ]
- [ ] Key 9: Trust God. [ ]

Look at the instructions for each key. How good are you at following each instruction? Try putting them into order, with your best at the top, and so on. For example, if you are good at using your mind, put it high on your list. If you are not so good at asking friends for advice, put that key low on your list.

Use the left-hand column of boxes for your list. Use the righthand column of boxes for a checkmark when you have read the appropriate pages.

Now start with the bottom item on your list, and turn to the relevant page.

Guidance is a relationship
Guidance is not a puzzle to be solved, but a relationship with Jesus. The closer we are to Jesus, the less anxious we will be about knowing God's will for our lives.

• "I am the true vine"
What relationship could be closer than the way a vine branch is linked to the main stem of the vine? Jesus said, "I am the true vine. ...Remain in me, and I will remain in you. ...I am the vine;

you are the branches. If a man remains in me and I in him, he will bear much fruit; apart from me you can do nothing."
John 15:1, 4-5

• A promise to hang on to
"God has said, 'Never will I leave you; never will I forsake you.'"
Hebrews 13:5

Key 1: Be humble

A proud person

A proud person may miss out on God's guidance simply through not being prepared to pray to God about it.

A characteristic of humility is to be contrite or repentant: "This is the one I esteem: he who is humble and contrite in spirit, and trembles at my word." *Isaiah 66:2*

Humility linked with ...

Seeking God	"Seek the LORD, all you humble."	*Zephaniah 2:3*
The meek	"I will leave within you the meek and humble, who trust in the name of the LORD."	*Zephaniah 3:12*
Gentleness	Jesus said, "I am gentle and humble in heart."	*Matthew 11:29*
Gentleness	"Be completely humble and gentle."	*Ephesians 4:2*
Other people	"In humility consider others better than yourselves."	*Philippians 2:3*

Blessings received by the humble

"The LORD *sustains* the humble."	*Psalm 147:6*
"[The LORD] *gives grace* to the humble."	*Proverbs 3:34*
"God opposes the proud but *gives grace* to the humble."	*1 Peter 5:5*
"Whoever humbles himself will be *exalted*."	*Matthew 23:12*
"I live in a high and holy place, but also with him who is contrite and lowly in spirit, *to revive the spirit* of the lowly and *to revive the heart* of the contrite."	*Isaiah 57:15*

The supreme example of humility – "he humbled himself"

"Your attitude should be the same as that of Christ Jesus:
Who, being in very nature God,
  did not consider equality with God something to be grasped,
but made himself nothing,
  taking the very nature of a servant,
  being made in human likeness.
And being found in appearance as a man,
  he humbled himself
  and became obedient to death – even death on a cross!"
Philippians 2:5-8

Concluding thought

"All of you, clothe yourselves with humility towards one
  another." *1 Peter 5:5*

Key 2: Pray

Dependence on God
Prayer shows dependence on God.

Who prayed in the Old Testament?

Person	Prayer	Bible reference
Abraham	For the city of Sodom	*Genesis 18:22-33*
Abraham's servant	For guidance	*Genesis 24:12-14*
Moses	A song of thanksgiving	*Exodus 15*
Hannah	For a son	*1 Samuel 1*
David	A song of thanksgiving	*2 Samuel 22*
Solomon	For wisdom	*1 Kings 3*
Nehemiah	For his nation	*Nehemiah 1*
Nebuchadnezzar	Praising God	*Daniel 4*
Jonah	A cry for help	*Jonah 2*
Habakkuk	For mercy	*Habakkuk 3*

Jesus in Gethsemane

"[Jesus] withdrew about a stone's throw beyond [his disciples], knelt down and prayed, *'Father, if you are willing, take this cup from me; yet not my will, but yours be done.'* An angel from heaven appeared to him and strengthened him. And being in anguish, he prayed more earnestly, and his sweat was like drops of blood falling to the ground." *Luke 22:41-44*

What position should we be in when we pray?

The Bible does not give any rules about whether we should sit, stand, or kneel to pray.

Kneeling

• Jesus sometimes knelt to pray. In the Garden of Gethsemane Jesus "knelt down and prayed" (*Luke 22:41*) and this may have given rise to the Christian custom of kneeling in prayer.

• At times, Paul knelt to pray. "For this reason I kneel before the Father." *Ephesians 3:14*

• Some of Paul's Christian friends knelt to pray.

"When [Paul] had said this, he knelt down with all of them and prayed." *Acts 20:36*

"All the disciples and their wives and children accompanied us out of the city, and there on the beach we knelt to pray." *Acts 21:5*

• Daniel prayed three times a day on his knees.

"Now when Daniel learned that the decree had been published, he went home to his upstairs room where the windows opened towards Jerusalem. Three times a day he got down on his knees and prayed, giving thanks to God, just has he had done before." *Daniel 6:10*

Daniel ended up being thrown to the lions because of this open worship of God.

Hands lifted up

"I want men everywhere to lift up holy hands in prayer, without anger or disputing." *1 Timothy 2:8*

Standing up

Jews stand up to pray. Solomon stood as he prayed. He also lifted up his hands as a indication that he was praying.

"Then Solomon stood before the altar of the LORD in front of the whole assembly of Israel, spread out his hands toward heaven and [prayed]." *1 Kings 8:21*

Hearts not bodies

The position of our bodies in prayer is not half so important as the attitude of our hearts. For "the LORD weighs the heart." *Proverbs 21:2*

Key 3: Follow the light you already have

A lamp, not a searchlight

God does not often give Christians "long-range" guidance about their future. It is more often just about the next step to take.

The psalmist said to God, "Your word is a lamp to my feet and a light for my path." *Psalm 119:105*

God's word was a "lamp" so he could see where he was walking, not a searchlight shining on his destination.

Do you really want to know the future?

It is not always to our advantage to know what is going to happen to us. Jesus told Peter, "When you are old you will stretch out your hands, and someone else will dress you and lead you where you do not want to go." *John 21:18*. This is probably a prediction of Peter's future martyrdom when, according to tradition, he would be killed by crucifixion.

We may be glad not to know all that will happen to us, later on in our lives.

What about other Christians?

We are not meant to pry into what God's will is for other Christians. Peter made this mistake.

> "Peter turned and saw that the disciple whom Jesus loved [John] was following them. ...When Jesus saw him he asked [Jesus], 'Lord, what about him?' Jesus answered, 'If I want him to remain alive until I return, what is that to you? You must follow me.'" *John 21:20-22*

We'll never know all we want to know

• The Bible never claims to tell us about everything.
• The Bible is primarily about salvation.
• The answers to what we need to know about salvation are found it its pages.
• "When he, the Spirit of truth, comes, he will guide you into all truth." *John 16:13*

Loving and obeying

Jesus said, "If anyone loves me, he will obey my teaching." *John 14:23*

It is often easier to be preoccupied with the future than to obey Jesus in the present.

Obedience and its links

Obedience linked with faith	*Romans 16:26*
Obedience linked with holiness	*Acts 26:18*
Obedience linked with righteousness	*Romans 6:13*
Obedience linked with God's blessing	*Deuteronomy 11:27*
Obedience linked with God's word	*Psalm 119:67*
Obedience linked with salvation	*Hebrews 5:9*

Key 4: Don't give up

Persevere

Jesus told two parables which both had the same moral to them. They were both aimed at encouraging his followers to keep praying.

Clearly, persevering in prayer is something that Christians have always found hard.

• The parable of the widow who wouldn't take "No" for an answer

"Then Jesus told his disciples a parable to show them that they should always pray and not give up. He said: 'In a certain town there was a judge who neither feared God nor cared about men. And there was a widow in that town who kept coming to him with the plea, "Grant me justice against my adversary."

'For some time he refused. But finally he said to himself, "Even though I don't fear God or care about men, yet because this widow keeps bothering me, I will see that she gets justice, so that she won't eventually wear me out with her coming!"'

And the Lord said, 'Listen to what the unjust judge says. And will not God bring about justice for his chosen ones, who cry out to him day and night? Will he keep putting them off? I tell you, he will see that they get justice, and quickly. However, when the Son of Man comes, will he find faith on the earth?'"
Luke 18:1-8

• The parable of the friend at midnight

"Then [Jesus] said to them, 'Suppose one of you has a friend, and he goes to him at midnight and says, "Friend, lend me three loaves of bread, because a friend of mine on a journey has come to me, and I have nothing to set before him."

'Then the one inside answers, "Don't bother me. The door is already locked, and my children are with me in bed. I can't get up and give you anything." I tell you, though he will not get up and give him the bread because he is his friend, yet because of the man's boldness he will get up and give him as much as he needs.'"
Luke 11:5-8

23

Keep on going

Perseverence is specifically needed by Christians seeking God's guidance for their lives.

Christians need to persevere in

• Running the Christian race. *Hebrews 12:1*
• Serving God. *Revelation 2:19*
• How they live and what they believe. *1 Timothy 4:16*
• Having confidence in God and doing his will.
Hebrews 10:35-36

Key 5: Don't be put off by barriers

A pioneer missionary with a tough skin

If Paul had been deflected from carrying out God's will in his life by the avalanche of events that happened to him, we would have been deprived of our greatest missionary and theologian.

Paul's trials

Paul left a record of some of the sufferings he gladly endured for the sake of Jesus, in 1 Corinthians 4:10-13 and 2 Corinthians 11:23-28.

- He was frequently imprisoned.
- He was severely flogged.
- He was exposed to death again and again.
- He received 195 lashes from the Jews alone.
- He was beaten three times with rods.
- He was stoned.
- He was shipwrecked.
- He spent a night and a day in the open sea.
- He was constantly on the move.
- He was in danger from rivers.
- He was in danger from bandits.
- He was in danger from his own countrymen.
- He was in danger from Gentiles.
- He was in danger in the city.
- He was in danger in the country.
- He was in danger at sea.
- He was in danger from false brethren.
- He experienced hunger, thirst, cold, and sometimes went around in rags.
- He was a fool for Christ's sake.
- He was dishonored.
- He was brutally treated.
- He was made homeless.
- He was cursed.
- He was persecuted.
- He was slandered.

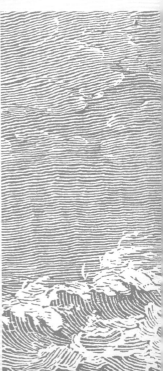

Setbacks

The setbacks we have experienced in our own lives become insignificant when compared with what some Christian missionaries and martyrs have suffered for Jesus.

Nevertheless, we all have our own problems: "For each one should carry his own load." *Galatians 6:5*

Helping others

The Bible tells us to help other people carry the loads which weigh them down and burden their lives: "Carry each other's burdens, and in this way you will fulfill the law of Christ." *Galatians 6:2*

A promise to hang on to

Jesus said, "And surely I am with you always, to the very end of the age." *Matthew 28:20*

Key 6:
Use your mind

Rational creatures
God made us with wonderful minds. We are meant to use them to the fullest – not least of all when it comes to finding out God's will for our lives.

Not like brute beasts
God promised the psalmist that his mind would be taught and informed:
"I will instruct you and teach you
in the way you should go;
I will counsel you and watch over you.
Do not be like the horse or the mule,
which have no understanding
but must be controlled by bit and bridle
or they will not come to you."
Psalm 32:8-9

Paul used his mind for God
Paul, the theologian, was a great strategist. He worked out how he would set about spreading the gospel of Jesus throughout the known world. He aimed mainly at centers of population, the cities.

• He debated
"[Paul] talked and debated with the Grecian Jews, but they tried to kill him." *Acts 9:29*
• He argued persuasively
"Paul entered the synagogue and spoke boldly there for three months, arguing persuasively about the kingdom of God."
Acts 19:8
• He reasoned
"[Paul] reasoned in the synagogues with the Jews and the God-fearing Greeks, as well as in the marketplace day by day."
Acts 17:17

Apollos used his mind for God too

"[Apollos] vigorously refuted the Jews in public debate, proving from the Scriptures that Jesus was the Christ." *Acts 18:28*

"Love the Lord with your mind"

• In the Old Testament we read: "Hear, O Israel...Love the LORD your God with all your heart and with all your soul and with all your strength." *Deuteronomy 6:4-5*
• In the New Testament we read: "Jesus replied: "Love the Lord your God with all your heart and with all your soul and with all your mind."" *Matthew 22:37*
• Peter
Peter wrote: "Prepare your minds for action." *1 Peter 1:13*

Key 7: Ask a friend

David and Jonathan
One of God's greatest gifts is friendship. "Jonathan became one in spirit with David, and he loved him as himself." *1 Samuel 18:1*

Ask a friend to pray for you
Ask a friend to pray that you may know God's guidance.
It can be quite a humbling experience to share personal prayer requests with a friend. Paul often asked his trusted Christian friends to pray for him.

Paul's requests for prayer

• Boldness to preach the gospel
"Pray also for me, that whenever I open my mouth, words may be given me so that I will fearlessly make known the mystery of the gospel, for which I am an ambassador in chains. Pray that I may declare it fearlessly, as I should." *Ephesians 6:19-20*
• Physical safety
"Pray that I may be rescued from the unbelievers in Judea." *Romans 15:31*

• Opportunity to preach about Jesus
"And pray for us, too, that God may open a door for our message, so that we may proclaim the mystery of Christ, for which I am in chains." *Colossians 4:3*
• General request for prayer
"Brothers, pray for us."
1 Thessalonians 5:25

Friends can get it wrong
Christian friends are not infallible.
Paul had to ignore the advice given to him by well-meaning Christians who urged him not to go to Jerusalem, even though their advice came "through the Spirit." *See Acts 21:4.*

Paul also prayed for his Christian friends

It seems that it was quite normal for Christians to ask for help from each other in this way in the early Church.

Paul prayed for:
• Christians at Colosse, so that they would have knowledge of God's will. *Colossians 1:9*
• Christians at Ephesus, so that they would be rooted in love. *Ephesians 3:17*
• Christians at Thessalonica, so that Jesus would be glorified in them. *2 Thessalonians 1:11-12*

A prayer for the Ephesians
"For this reason I kneel before the Father, from whom his whole family in heaven and on earth derives its name. I pray that out of his glorious riches he may strengthen you with power through his Spirit in your inner being, so that Christ may dwell in your hearts through faith. And I pray that you, being rooted and established in love, may have power, together with all the saints, to grasp how wide and long and high and deep is the love of Christ, and to know this love that surpasses knowlege – that you may be filled to the measure of all the fulness of God." *Ephesians 3:14-19*

See also: *Trusting God does not mean we don't need friends!*, page 12

Key 8: Remember, God is not in a hurry

God's timescale

God's view of time and our view of time are often very different.

We tend to be in a rush to achieve things, but God is never in a hurry.

Peter writes: "Dear friends: with the Lord a day is like a thousand years, and a thousand years are like a day." *2 Peter 3:8*

Before time

Before time, as we know it, God was active.

In creation	"In the beginning God created the heavens."	*Genesis 1:1*
In choosing us	"[God] chose us in him before the creation of the world."	*Ephesians 1:4*

A time for everything

The writer of the Book of Ecclesiastes emphasizes that everything happens at God's appointed time.

A time for ...

"There is a time for everything,
and a season for every activity under heaven:
a time to be born and a time to die,
a time to plant and a time to uproot,
a time to kill and a time to heal,
a time to tear down and a time to build,
a time to weep and a time to laugh,
a time to mourn and a time to dance,
a time to scatter stones and a time to gather them,
a time to embrace and a time to refrain,
a time to search and a time to give up,
a time to keep and a time to throw away,
a time to tear and a time to mend,
a time to be silent and a time to speak,
a time to love and a time to hate,
a time for war and a time for peace."
Ecclesiastes 3:1-8

God is your creator

"Remember your Creator in the days of your youth." *Ecclesiastes 12:1*

Key 9: Trust God

Daniel's three friends

Shadrach, Meshach and Abednego are fine examples of people who completely trusted God. When they were about to be thrown into a fiery furnace, for not bowing down and worshipping King Nebuchadnezzar's image of gold, they said to the king:

> "O Nebuchadnezzar, we do not need to defend ourselves before you in this matter. If we are thrown into the blazing furnace, the God we serve is able to save us from it, and he will rescue us from your hand, O king. But even if he does not, we want you to know, O king, that we will not serve your gods or worship the image of gold you have set up." *Daniel 3:16-18*

Trusting God

When to trust God
- At all times. "Trust in him at all times, O people." *Psalm 62:8*

How to trust God
- With all your heart. "Trust in the LORD with all your heart and lean not on your own understanding." *Proverbs 3:5*
- In quietness. "In quietness and trust is your strength." *Isaiah 30:15*

Why trust God?
- Because of God's unfailing love. "But I trust in your unfailing love." *Psalm 13:5*

The result of trusting God
- Lack of fear. "I will trust and not be afraid." *Isaiah 12:2*
- God's care. "He cares for those who trust in him." *Nahum 1:7*
- Safety. "Whoever trusts in the LORD is kept safe." *Proverbs 29:25*

What should not be trusted
- Chariots (representing human power). "Some trust in chariots." *Psalm 20:7*
- Gold (representing human wealth). "If I have put my trust in gold." *Job 31:24*
- Extortion. "Do not trust in extortion." *Psalm 62:10*
- Deceptive words. "Do not trust in deceptive words." *Jeremiah 7:4*

Prayers for approaching death
The dying prayers of Jesus and Stephen express their trust in God.
- As Jesus hung dying on the cross, he prayed: "Father, into your hands I commit my spirit." *Luke 23:46*
- As Stephen was being stoned to death, he prayed: "Lord Jesus, receive my spirit." *Acts 7:59*

A promise to hang on to
"Cast all your anxiety on [God] because he cares for you."
1 Peter 5:7

Visions and dreams

The Old Testament
God's will was often revealed to people through their dreams.

People in the Old Testament who had special dreams

Jacob in Bethel	*Genesis 28:12*
Joseph	*Genesis 37:5-11*
Jacob in Haran	*Genesis 31:10-13*
A Midianite soldier	*Judges 7:13*
Solomon in Gibeon	*1 Kings 3:5*
Nebuchadnezzar	*Daniel 2*
Daniel	*Daniel 7:1*

Dreams surrounding Jesus' birth and early years
Jesus was protected in his early years through the dreams of his foster father, Joseph.

• **Dream number one**
"The Lord appeared to [Joseph] in a dream and said, 'Joseph son of David, do not be afraid to take Mary home as your wife, because what is conceived in her is from the Holy Spirit.'" *Matthew 1:20*

• **Dream number two**
"An angel of the Lord appeared to Joseph in a dream. 'Get up,' he said, 'take the child and his mother and escape to Egypt. Stay there until I tell you, for Herod is going to search for the child to kill him.'" *Matthew 2:13*

• **Dream number three**
"After Herod died, an angel of the Lord appeared in a dream to Joseph in Egypt and said, 'Get up, take the child and his mother and go to the land of Israel, for those who were trying to take the child's life are dead.'" *Matthew 2:19-20*

Joseph's obedience
We may feel that it was easy for Joseph. After all, he was told exactly what to do in his dreams. But he still had to do the hard part – obey God's will. "To obey is better than sacrifice."
1 Samuel 15:22

Beware
- "Much dreaming and many words are meaningless. Therefore stand in awe of God." *Ecclesiastes 5:7*
- Jeremiah wrote: "I have heard what the prophets say who prophesy lies in my name. They say, 'I had a dream! I had a dream!'" *Jeremiah 23:25*

Visions and dreams
Visions were revelations from God, which occurred while the prophet was in a dream-like state. *See Genesis 46:2; Luke 1:22.*

Visions were another important way God gave directions to people. God used dreams as a way of revealing his will, but dreams were to be tested against *written* revelation. *See Deuteronomy 13:1-5.*

God said to Miriam and Aaron,
"When a prophet of the LORD is among you,
I reveal myself to him in visions,
I speak to him in dreams."
Numbers 12:6

Paul's vision
"During the night Paul had a vision of a man of Macedonia standing and begging him, 'Come over to Macedonia and help us.' After Paul had seen the vision, we got ready at once to leave for Macedonia, concluding that God had called us to preach the gospel to them." *Acts 16:9-10*

This vision resulted in the gospel being preached in Europe for the first time.

The hardest part – waiting

Waiting "for" and waiting "on"

Waiting for guidance is often a very tough experience. This time can be used positively to wait on God:

"The LORD is good to everyone who trusts in him,
So it is best for us to wait in patience."
Lamentations 3:25 RSV

Patience is a fruit of the Spirit

"The fruit of the Spirit is love, joy, peace, patience, kindness, goodness, faithfulness, gentleness and self-control." *Galatians 5:22-23*

Patience is one of the most necessary Christian qualities, when God's guidance seems hard to find or difficult to follow.

Christians are told: "Be patient with everyone."
1 Thessalonians 5:14

Christians need patience for

• Facing trials
"The testing of your faith develops perseverance. Perseverance must finish its work so that you may be mature and complete, not lacking anything."
James 1:3-4

• Enduring persecution
"If when you do right and suffer for it you take it patiently, you have God's approval." *1 Peter 2:20 RSV*

• Living each day for Jesus
"Let us throw off everything that hinders and the sin that so easily entangles, and let us run with perseverance the race marked out for us." *Hebrews 12:1*

• Receiving God's promises
"You need to persevere so that when you have done the will of God, you will receive what he has promised." *Hebrews 10:36*

• Waiting for Jesus' return
"Be patient, then, brothers, until the Lord's coming." *James 5:7*

A promise to hang on to
"Blessed are all who wait for [the Lord]."
Isaiah 30:18

What to do when God seems distant

God "speaks" to Elijah
Elijah found that God "spoke" to him in a most unexpected way – in hushed tones.

Not in the wind, earthquake or fire
"The LORD said [to Elijah], 'Go and stand on the mountain in the presence of the LORD, for the LORD is about to pass by.'

Then a great and powerful wind tore the mountains apart and shattered the rocks before the LORD, but the LORD was not in the wind. After the wind there was an earthquake, but the LORD was not in the earthquake. After the earthquake came a fire, but the LORD was not in the fire. And after the fire came a gentle whisper. When Elijah heard it, he pulled his cloak over his face and went out and stood at the mouth of the cave."
1 Kings 19:11-13

Finding the meaning of God's silences
If God seems far away, it is not necessarily a sign that we have done anything wrong or that we are being punished by him. It may be because:

• God has spoken but we have paid no attention.
"But since you rejected me when I called
and no one gave heed when I stretched out my hand."
Proverbs 1:24

• He is confounding the powerful and proud.

"[Herod] plied [Jesus] with many questions, but Jesus gave him no answer." *Luke 23:9*

• He is testing our faith in Jesus.

"A Canaanite woman ... came to [Jesus], crying out, 'Lord, Son of David, have mercy on me! My daughter is suffering terribly from demon-possession.' Jesus did not answer a word." *Matthew 15:22-23*

(The next verses show how Jesus' silence drew out the woman's faith. Jesus then went on to heal her daughter.)

When God seems far away from us

In the Old Testament, many of God's followers had such an experience, and through it came closer to God.

The psalmist pleads with God, "Do not hide your face from me." This possibility made him redouble his efforts to seek God. "My heart says of you, 'Seek his face!' Your face, Lord, I will seek." *Psalm 27:8-9*

What to do
when you let God down

When things go wrong
If things go wrong, it is easy to allow a situation to go from bad to worse. When we've let God down once, it becomes easy to do it again and again, if we are not careful.

Forbidden
The Bible makes it quite clear that we should never seek God's will through any occult practices.

> "When you enter the land the LORD your God is giving you, do not learn to imitate the detestable ways of the nations there. Let no one be found among you who sacrifices his son or daughter in the fire, who practices divination or sorcery, interprets omens, engages in witchcraft, or casts spells, or who is a medium or spiritist or who consults the dead. Anyone who does these things is detestable to the LORD, and because of these detestable practices the LORD your God will drive out those nations before you.
> You must be blameless before the Lord your God."
> *Deuteronomy 18:9-13*

Saul and David compared

Saul
When things went particularly poorly for Saul, he turned to a medium.

• **Saul's mistake**
"Saul then said to his attendants, "Find me a woman who is a medium, so that I may go and inquire of her."" *1 Samuel 28:7 (The whole story is in 1 Samuel 28:6-25)*

• **Saul's epitaph**
"Saul died because he was unfaithful to the LORD; he did not keep the word of the LORD, and even consulted a medium for guidance, and did not inquire of the LORD. So the LORD put him to death and turned the kingdom over to David son of Jesse." *1 Chronicles 10:13-14*

Footnote David is remembered as God's most faithful king of Israel. "The LORD has sought out a man after his own heart." *1 Samuel 13:14.* David became such a person.

David

David, in severe difficulties, turned back to God.

• David's sins

David had committed adultery with Bathsheba. He then arranged for Bathsheba's husband, Uriah, to be killed in battle. See 2 Samuel 11–12. What could an adulterer and murderer do about this situation?

• David's return

We have a record of what David did. He confessed his sin to God.

"Have mercy on me, O God,
  according to your unfailing love;
according to your great compassion
  blot out my transgressions.
Wash away all my iniquity
  and cleanse me from my sin.
For I know my transgressions,
  and my sin is always before me.
Against you, you only, have I sinned
  and done what is evil in your
    sight."
Psalm 51:1-4

A promise to hang on to

• "If we confess our sins, [God] is faithful and just and will forgive us our sins and purify us from all unrighteousness." *1 John 1:9*

What to do when you're at your wits' end

Talk to yourself

The first sign of madness is *not* talking to yourself!

The psalmist often spoke to himself about his spiritual state: "My soul is downcast within me; therefore I will remember you [God]." *Psalm 42:6*

Honesty is the best policy

Nobody rejoiced in God more than the psalmist. But he also was honest enough to give voice to the times when he was feeling very low.

"Deep calls to deep
in the roar of your waterfalls;
all your waves and breakers
have swept over me."
Psalm 42:7

It's as if the psalmist is saying, "If you feel low, tell God about it, and admit it to yourself."

Questions and answers

Here are two questions the psalmist asked himself, and the answers he came up with, in Psalm 42.

- "Why are you downcast, O my soul? ... Put your hope in God."
- "Why so disturbed within me? ... I will yet praise him, my Savior and my God."

Turn to prayer

When we are down, we can turn to prayer, even though it may be the last thing we feel like doing.

Some reminders about prayer from the Psalms

- God loves to hear our prayers.
"God has surely listened
and heard my voice in prayer.
Praise be to God,
who has not rejected my prayer
or withheld his love from me!"
Psalm 66:19-20

- Praise God for his love to you.
"Praise be to the LORD,
for he showed his wonderful
love to me."
Psalm 31:21

- Praise God for his greatness.
"I will praise you, O LORD, among
the nations;
I will sing of you among the
peoples.
For great is your love, reaching to
the heavens;
your faithfulness reaches to the
skies."
Psalm 57:9-10

- Tell God how great he is!
"As for God, his way is perfect;
the word of the LORD is flawless.
He is a shield
for all who take refuge in him.
For who is God besides the LORD?
And who is the Rock except our
God?"
Psalm 18:30-31

A promise to hang on to

"I guide you in the way of wisdom
and lead you along straight paths."
Proverbs 4:11

Time to make up your mind

Introduction

How do we decide on whether things are right or wrong, when there is nothing about them in the Ten Commandments? Where there is no one verse in the Bible to refer to, we have to try and see what the Bible's general teaching on the subject is. We should also find out whether Jesus gave any teaching on the subject.

Should I drink alcohol?

Christians vary in their answer to this question. Some say, "I never touch a drop." They have a very strong conviction that they should never drink a drop of alcohol, and even have unfermented grape juice, in place of wine, when they take part in the Lord's Supper.

Others ask, "What's wrong with a glass of wine with a meal, or having a drink at a party?"

Looking for the answer

• **Don't get drunk**
This is clearly taught in the Bible: "Do not get drunk on wine." *Ephesians 5:18*

• **Wine is a gift from God**
"[God] makes grass grow for the cattle,
and plants for man to cultivate –
bringing forth food from the earth:
wine that gladdens the heart of man,
oil to make his face shine,
and bread that sustains his heart."
Psalm 104:14-15

• **Wine as a medicine**
Paul tells his young friend, Timothy, who seems to have had a weak constitution: "Stop drinking only water, and use a little wine because of your stomach and your frequent illnesses." *1 Timothy 5:23*

Reaching different conclusions

In matters in which a vital principle of the Christain faith is not at stake, it is important that Christians do not expend a lot of energy on arguing with other Christians who hold different opinions to them.

Paul tried to prevent Christians from arguing with each other in this way:

"One man considers one day more sacred than another; another man considers every day alike. Each one should be fully convinced in his own mind. He who regards one day as special, does so to the Lord. He who eats meat, eats to the Lord, for he gives thanks to God; and he who abstains, does so to the Lord and gives thanks to God. For none of us lives to himself alone and none of us dies to himself alone. If we live, we live to the Lord; and if we die, we die to the Lord. So, whether we live or die, we belong to the Lord."
Romans 14:5-8

Should I gamble?

Bible principle to bear in mind: hard work is commended.

"If a man will not work, he shall not eat." *2 Thessalonians 3:10*

Is it okay to live together before marriage?

Bible principle to bear in mind: sexual immorality is decried.

Fornication is used figuratively to represent spiritual unfaithfulness to God:

"The body is not meant for sexual immorality, but for the Lord, and the Lord for the body. ... Flee from sexual immorality. All other sins a man commits are outside his body, but he who sins sexually sins against his own body."
1 Corinthians 6:13b, 18

Should I watch adult movies and videos?

Bible principle to bear in mind: our minds should be fed with uplifting thoughts and attitudes.

"Finally brothers, whatever is true, whatever is noble, whatever is right, whatever is pure, whatever is lovely, whatever is admirable – if anything is excellent or praiseworthy – think about such things." *Philippians 4:8*

"... I tell you that anyone who looks lustfully at a woman has already committed adultery with her in his heart." *Matthew 5:28*

Should I marry a non-Christian?

Do not be unequally yoked

The key verse many Christians turn to, when they are concerned about a Christian marrying a non-Christian, is: "Do not be yoked together with unbelievers." The King James Version translates this as "Be not unequally yoked …"
2 Corinthians 6:14

In this verse, Paul is saying that to be closely partnered with an unbeliever is like trying to plough a field with two incompatible animals – like having an ox and a donkey hitched up together!

This verse says nothing about marriage. It could be applied to a close business partnership between a Christian and a non-Christian. But it is often cited as the reason Christians should not marry non-Christians.

The verses in 2 Corinthians 6:14-16 ask two other questions:
• What do righteousness and wickedness have in common?
• What harmony is there between Christ and Belial (another word for Satan)?

Remember *who* God is

During times when we feel that we don't want to hear what God says, what should we do? How should we react if we do not want to seek out God's guidance on some very personal matter?

We must remember that God wants the very best for us. And this comes from following his guidance.

Three Hebrew words

The way God guides us is seen in three Hebrew words:

• Nahag

This word means "to conduct along a path." God led the people of Israel out of their slavery in Egypt in this way.

"By day the LORD went ahead of them in a pillar of cloud to guide them on their way and by night in a pillar of fire to give them light, so that they could travel by day or night." *Exodus 13:21*

• Darak

This word means "to walk, to travel." The psalmist prayed that God would guide him in ways that would please God.

"Show me your ways, O LORD, teach me your paths;
guide me in your truth and teach me,
for you are God my Savior, and my hope all day long."
Psalm 25:4-5

• Nahal

This word means "to lead with care." It is the word used of a shepherd looking after his sheep. Isaiah the prophet comforted God's people when they thought that God had forsaken them.

"He tends his flock like a shepherd:
He gathers the lambs in his arms
and carries them close to his heart;
he gently leads those that have young."
Isaiah 40:11

47

Should I give my money to the poor?

Give a tenth of your income

In the Old Testament, God's people were told to give a tenth of their income for God's work, and for the poor. This instruction is not repeated in the New Testament.

So, should we give more or less than this?

Paul's advice

Paul outlines how we are to give money, and writes, "Each man should give what he has decided in his heart to give, not reluctantly or under compulsion, for God loves a cheerful giver." *2 Corinthians 9:7*

• Give it some thought.
• Do not give grudgingly.
• Give without being forced into doing it.
• Give cheerfully.

Giving everything away

This seems to have happened, on at least one occasion, in the early Church. "All the believers were together and had everything in common. Selling their possessions and goods, they gave to anyone as he had need." *Acts 2:44-45*

So, while there is no hint of this being compulsory, it certainly took place.

Jesus advises a rich young man

"As Jesus started on his way, a man ran up to him and fell on his knees before him. 'Good teacher,' he asked, 'what must I do to inherit eternal life?'

'Why do you call me good?' Jesus answered. 'No one is good – except God alone. You know the commandments: "Do not murder, do not commit adultery, do not steal, do not give false testimony, do not defraud, honor your father and mother."'

'Teacher,' he declared, 'all these I have kept since I was a boy.'

Jesus looked at him and loved him. 'One thing you lack,' he said. 'Go, sell everything you have and give to the poor, and you will have treasure in heaven. Then come, follow me.'"
Mark 10:17-21

Points to note

Jesus did not say this to every person he met. Clearly this rich man needed to hear this from Jesus so he could see that his money was more important to him than God's kingdom.

A sad ending

"At this the man's face fell. He went away sad, because he had great wealth. Jesus looked around and said to his disciples, 'How hard it is for the rich to enter the kingdom of God!'"
Mark 10:22-23

What to do when God's answer is "No"

God's answers

God answers all prayers. The answer may be "Yes," "No," or "Wait."

The apostle Paul was given the answer "No" to one of his prayers. He had some kind of illness, which he called his "thorn in the flesh." Paul prayed and prayed that God would heal him make him well.

> "To keep me from becoming conceited because of these surpassingly great revelations, there was given me a thorn in my flesh, a messenger of Satan, to torment me. Three times I pleaded with the Lord to take it away from me. But he said to me, 'My grace is sufficient for you, for my power is made perfect in weakness.' Therefore I will boast all the more gladly about my weaknesses, so that Christ's power may rest on me." *2 Corinthians 12:7-9*

Bad times

When things are tough, or when things go wrong, it is even more important to know how one should behave as a Christian.

Continue to seek God's guidance

This needs faith. "And without faith it is impossible to please God, because anyone who comes to him must believe that he exists and that he rewards those who earnestly seek him." *Hebrews 11:6*

Be willing to do God's will

If we want to do something that we know is not God's will, it can be quite a severe test of our faith. If this happens, we need to choose to do God's will. Jesus said, "If anyone chooses to do God's will, he will find out whether my teaching comes from God or whether I speak of my own." *John 7:17*

Do not doubt God

Can we follow God's will for us without question?

"But when he asks, he must believe and not doubt, because he who doubts is like a wave of the sea, blown and tossed by the wind. That man should not think he will receive anything from the Lord; he is a double-minded man, unstable in all he does."
James 1:6-7

"You won't be heard, just because you pray a lot!"

There is a middle ground between persisting in prayer, and praying endlessly for the sake of it. Jesus once warned people about their long prayers.

"When you pray, do not keep on babbling like pagans, for they think they will be heard because of their many words. Do not be like them, for your Father knows what you need before you ask him."
Matthew 6:7-8

See also: *What to do when God seems distant*, page 38.

Five classic ways in which God guides

The classic guides

On pages 54-63, five classic ways of finding God's will are set out.

- God guides through inner conviction.
- God guides through prayer.
- God guides through circumstances.
- God guides through the Bible.
- God guides in unexpected ways.

52

Casting lots

In Bible times, one way people received God's guidance was by casting lots. Lots were two-sided discs. The way they landed when thrown was believed to denote God's will. In the Old Testament, land was divided up in this way. Lots were also used in the law courts. *See Joshua 18:10.*

"Casting the lot settles disputes and keeps strong opponents apart." *Proverbs 18:18*

Matthias was chosen as a replacement apostle for Judas by casting lots.

"Then they cast lots, and the lot fell to Matthias; so he was added to the eleven apostles." *Acts 1:26*

Urim and Thummin

The Jews had sacred lots called Urim and Thummin. These sacred lots were used by the high priest to find out God's will, especially in times of crisis.

"Also put the Urim and the Thummin in the breastpiece, so they may be over Aaron's heart whenever he enters the presence of the LORD. Thus Aaron will always bear the means of making decisions for the Israelites over his heart before the LORD." *Exodus 28:30*

"[Joshua] is to stand before Eleazar the priest, who will obtain decisions before him by inquiring of the Urim before the LORD." *Numbers 27:21*

53

Classic guide 1: God guides through inner conviction

The Holy Spirit as guide

The most important "inner" guide a Christian can have is the Holy Spirit. Jesus promised his first followers that "the Spirit of truth" would guide them "into all truth." *John 16:13*

- God's Spirit is in every Christian.
  "No one can say, 'Jesus is Lord,' except by the Holy Spirit." *1 Corinthians 12:3*

- God's Spirit makes God's will known to us.
  "But the Counselor, the Holy Spirit, whom the Father will send in my name, will teach you all things and will remind you of everything I have said to you." *John 14:26*

Conscience

Inner conviction should come from an educated conscience, not blind prejudice. Our thoughts, feelings, and conscience all need to be informed and molded by God's teaching from the Bible. Unless this happens, we may hold the strongest convictions in the world, but that in itself does not make us right.

- Obtaining an "educated" conscience
"Oh, how I love your law!
  I meditate on it all day long.
Your commands make me wiser
      than my enemies,
  for they are ever with me.
I have more insight than all my
      teachers,
  for I meditate on your statutes."
Psalm 119:97-99

Different types of conscience

- A weak conscience
Christians must look after those who have weak consciences, and prevent difficulties and temptations from being put in their way.
  "If anyone with a weak conscience sees you who have this knowledge eating in an idol's temple, won't he be emboldened to eat what has been sacrificed to idols? ... When you sin against your brothers in this way and wound their weak conscience, you sin against Christ." *1 Corinthians 8:10-12*

- A seared conscience
There are false teachers who deliberately try to turn Christians away from following Jesus, to evil paths.
  "The Spirit clearly says that in later times some will abandon the faith and follow deceiving spirits and things taught by demons.

55

Such teachings come through hypocritical liars, whose consciences have been seared as with a hot iron." *1 Timothy 4:1-2*

• A cleansed conscience
"How much more, then, will the blood of Christ, who through the eternal Spirit offered himself unblemished to God, cleanse our consciences from acts that lead to death, so that we may serve the living God!" *Hebrews 9:14*

• A clear conscience
"But do this with gentleness and respect, keeping a clear conscience, so that those who speak maliciously against your good behavior in Christ may be ashamed of their slander."
1 Peter 3:15-16

• A good conscience
"Paul looked straight at the Sanhedrin and said, "My brothers, I have fulfilled my duty to God in all good conscience to this day."" *Acts 23:1*

A promise to hang on to
"The LORD will guide you always;
    he will satisfy your needs in a
    sun-scorched land
    and will strengthen your frame.
You will be like a well-watered
    garden,
    like a spring whose waters never
    fail."
Isaiah 58:11

Classic guide 2: God guides through prayer

Heart and prayer

We might infer from the Bible that it is not the length of our prayers, the position in which we pray, the words we use in our prayers, or whether our prayers are sung, said or unspoken that matter most. It is the state of our heart that counts. "In your hearts set apart Christ as Lord." *1 Peter 3:15*

Preparing hearts for prayer

• We need forgiven hearts
"He who conceals his sins does
　　not prosper,
　but whoever confesses and
　　renounces them finds mercy."
Proverbs 28:13

• We need humble hearts
"The sacrifices of God are a
　　broken spirit;
　a broken and a contrite heart,
　O God, you will not despise."
Psalm 51:17

• We need obedient hearts
"Those who obey [Jesus']
commands live in him, and he in
them." *1 John 3:24*

• We need forgiving hearts
As he was being stoned to death,
"[Stephen] fell on his knees and
cried out, 'Lord, do not hold this
sin against them.'" *Acts 7:60*

Prayer requests

Jesus taught people to pray on their own, and to pray with others and for others.

"Again, I tell you that if two of you on earth agree about anything you ask for, it will be done for you by my Father in heaven. For where two or three come together in my name, there am I with them." *Matthew 18:19-20*

The power of group prayer in the Acts of the Apostles

• Before the Holy Spirit came
"They all joined together constantly in prayer, along with the women and Mary the mother of Jesus, and with his brothers." *Acts 1:14*

• "Set" forms of prayers
"They devoted themselves to the apostles' teaching and to the fellowship, to the breaking of bread and to prayer." *Acts 2:42*

• Prayer that shook the room
"After they prayed, the place where they were meeting was shaken." *Acts 4:31*

• A commissioning service
"So after they had fasted and prayed, they placed their hands on them and sent them off." *Acts 13:3*

Pray without ceasing

There is no place, or time, when you cannot pray.

Paul told his Christian friends at Thessalonica about one of the "secrets" of prayer – to pray all the time!

"Pray continually; give thanks in all circumstances." *1 Thessalonians 5:17-18*

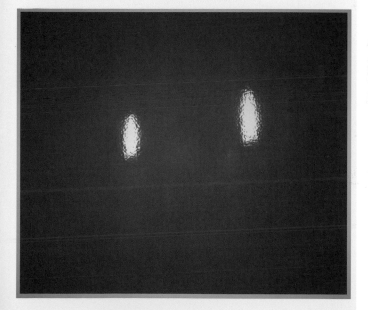

Classic guide 3: God guides through circumstances

Guidance and common sense

There's nothing wrong in being guided by common sense. God guided Paul through many seemingly ordinary situations.

How God guided Paul in "common sense" ways

• Bitten by a poisonous snake
"Paul gathered a pile of brushwood and, as he put it on the fire, a viper, driven out by the heat, fastened itself on his hand. When the islanders saw the snake hanging from his hand, they said to each other, "This man must be a murderer."" *Acts 28:3-4*

What did Paul do?
"Paul shook the snake off into the fire and suffered no ill-effects." *Acts 28:5*

• Fall from a window
"Paul spoke to the people and, because he intended to leave the next day, kept on talking until midnight. There were many lamps in the upstairs room where we were meeting. Seated in a window was a young man named Eutychus, who was sinking into a deep sleep as Paul talked on and on. When he was sound asleep, he fell to the ground from the third storey and was picked up dead." *Acts 20:7-9*

What did Paul do?
"Paul went down, threw himself on the young man and put his arms around him. 'Don't be alarmed,' he said. 'He's alive!' ... The people took the young man home alive and were greatly comforted." *Acts 20:10-12*

One of Paul's mottoes
"To the Jews I became like a Jew, to win the Jews. ...To those not having the law I became like one not having the law. ... I have become all things to all men so that by all possible means I might save some." *1 Corinthians 9:20-22*

One of Paul's strong beliefs
"We know that in all things God works for the good of those who love him, who have been called according to his purpose." *Romans 8:28*

• The trial
Paul was on trial before two groups of people, the Pharisees and the Sadducees.

What did Paul do?
He managed to set his opponents against each other with his opening line of defence:
"Paul [facing the supreme Jewish court], knowing that some of them were Sadducees and the others Pharisees, called out in the Sanhedrin, 'My brothers, I am a Pharisee, the son of a Pharisee. I stand on trial because of my hope in the resurrection of the dead.' When he said this, a dispute broke out between the Pharisees and the Sadducees, and the assembly was divided. (The Sadducees say that there is no resurrection, and that there are neither angels nor spirits, but the Pharisees acknowledge them all.)
There was a great uproar, and some of the teachers of the law who were Pharisees stood up and argued vigorously. 'We find nothing wrong with this man,' they said."
Acts 23:6-9

• A plot to kill Paul
"The next morning the Jews formed a conspiracy and bound themselves with an oath not to eat or drink until they had killed Paul. More than forty men were involved in this plot. They went to the chief priests and elders and said, 'We have taken a solemn oath not to eat anything until we have killed Paul. Now then, you and the Sanhedrin petition the commander to bring him before you on the pretext of wanting more accurate information about his case. We are ready to kill him before he gets here.'
But when the son of Paul's sister heard of this plot, he went into the barracks and told Paul."
Acts 23:12-16

What did Paul do?
"Then Paul called one of the centurions and said, 'Take this young man to the commander; he has something to tell him.' So he took him to the commander."
Acts 23:17
(This resulted in Paul being given an escort of "two hundred soldiers, seventy horsemen and two hundred spearmen."
Acts 23:23)

Classic guide 4: God guides through the Bible

The correct focus
Probably the greatest mistake we make about seeking God's will in our lives is to focus on ourselves instead of focusing on God.
- God exists. *Hebrews 11:6*
- God has a plan and purpose for our lives. *Jeremiah 1:4-5*
- God wants us to know about his plan. *Isaiah 30:21*

Right and wrong
One of the functions of the Bible is to tell us God's thoughts about right and wrong, and how we should think and behave.
- "The words of the LORD are flawless." *Psalm 12:6*
- "All Scripture is God-breathed and is useful for teaching, rebuking, correcting and training in righteousness, so that the man of God may be thoroughly equipped for every good work." *2 Timothy 3:16-17*

Commit your way to the Lord
One of the most helpful passages about guidance concerns committing ourselves to God. Notice the commands used in the following verses from Psalm 37: "Trust," "Delight," "Be still," "Wait patiently," and "Do not fret."

Psalm 37
"Trust in the LORD and do good,
  dwell in the land and enjoy safe pasture.
Delight yourself in the LORD
  and he will give you the desires of your heart.
Commit your way to the LORD;
  trust in him and he will do this:
He will make your righteousness shine like the dawn,
  the justice of your cause like the noonday sun.
Be still before the LORD and wait patiently for him;
  do not fret when men succeed in their ways,
  when they carry out their wicked schemes."
Psalm 37:3-7

Psalm 119

Just about all of the 176 verses of this psalm tell us something about God's word. The psalm uses eight different words to tell us the same basic thing.

• **Law**

"Blessed are they whose ways are
     blameless,
   who walk according to the law of
     the LORD."
Psalm 119:1

"In the night I remember your
     name, O LORD,
   and I will keep your law."
Psalm 119:55

• **Statutes**

"Blessed are they who keep his
     statutes
   and seek him with all their
     heart."
Psalm 119:2

• **Precepts**

"You have laid down precepts
that are to be fully obeyed."
Psalm 119:4

• **Commands**

"I seek you with all my heart;
   do not let me stray from your
     commands."
Psalm 119:10

• **Decrees**

"You are good, and what you do
     is good;
   teach me your decrees."
Psalm 119:68

• **Word**

"How can a young man keep
     his way pure?
   By living according to your
     word."
Psalm 119:9

Classic guide 5: God guides in unexpected ways!

Balaam's donkey

Balaam's donkey must be about the most unusual way God used to guide anyone! A talking donkey, a disobedient prophet and an angel are the three participants in the story.

"When the donkey saw the angel of the LORD, she lay down under Balaam, and he was angry and beat her with his staff. Then the LORD opened the donkey's mouth, and she said to Balaam, 'What have I done to you to make you beat me these three times?'" *Numbers 22:27-28*

Balaam left this amazing incident, knowing that he now had to follow God's ways, with words from the angel ringing in his ear:

"Go ... but speak only what I tell you." *Numbers 22:35*

The Holy Spirit and the unexpected

In the New Testament God provided guidance through the Holy Spirit, but the 'means' by which this guidance came is not always mentioned. Much of the Holy Spirit's guidance was also most unexpected. It's almost if we are being taught to expect the unexpected.

Jesus

Jesus went into the desert to be tempted.

"Jesus, full of the Holy Spirit, returned from the Jordan and was led by the Spirit in the desert, where for forty days he was tempted by the Devil." *Luke 4:1-2*

Paul

Paul knew he would face serious dangers if he went to Jerusalem.

"And now, compelled by the Spirit, I am going to Jerusalem, not knowing what will happen to me there. I only know that in every city the Holy Spirit warns me that prison and hardships are facing me." *Acts 20:22-23*

All Christians

"Those who are led by the Spirit of God are children of God." *Romans 8:14*

The barriers of prejudice are smashed

Prejudice is hard to break. As a Jew, Peter was brought up to have little regard for non-Jews, Gentiles. No wonder it took an unexpected revelation to change Peter's thinking.

"[Peter] saw heaven opened and something like a large sheet being let down to earth by its four corners. It contained all kinds of four-footed animals, as well as reptiles of the earth and birds of the air. Then a voice told him, 'Get up, Peter. Kill and eat.'

'Surely not, Lord!' Peter replied. "I have never eaten anything impure or unclean.'

The voice spoke to him a second time, 'Do not call anything impure that God has made clean.'" *Acts 10:11-15*

This led Peter to do what he had previously thought was quite wrong. He went to the house of a Gentile, Cornelius the Roman centurion, and told his whole household about Jesus.

Can God "guide" me to do wrong?

David's temptation

David is tempted and encouraged to harm King Saul, who is trying to capture and kill him. But David refuses to kill Saul, even though he has opportunities to do it.

• David's story

"The men said, 'This is the day the LORD spoke of when he said to you, "I will give your enemy into your hands for you to deal with as you wish."' Then David crept up unnoticed and cut off a corner of Saul's robe.

Afterwards, David was conscience-stricken for having cut off a corner of his robe. He said to his men, 'The LORD forbid that I should do such a thing to my master, the LORD's anointed, or lift my hand against him; for he is the anointed of the LORD.'"

1 Samuel 24:4-6

God's guidance is ...

• For ever

"For this God is our God for ever and ever;
  he will be our guide even to the end."
Psalm 48:14

• On peaceful ways

"[You will] guide our feet into the path of peace."
Luke 1:79

• With his counsel

"You guide me with your counsel, and afterwards you will take me into glory."
Psalm 73:24

• On what is right

"He guides the humble in what is right
  and teaches them his way."
Psalm 25:9